The

SUPERNATURAL

SKYLINE

The

SUPERNATURAL SKYLINE

Where Heaven Touches Earth

JIM HYLTON

DESTINY IMAGE® PUBLISHERS, INC.

P.O. Box 310, Shippensburg, PA 17257-0310

"Speaking to the Purposes of God for This Generation and for the Generations to Come."

This book and all other Destiny Image, Revival Press, MercyPlace, Fresh Bread, Destiny Image Fiction, and Treasure House books are available at Christian bookstores and distributors worldwide.

For a U.S. bookstore nearest you, call 1-800-722-6774.

For more information on foreign distributors, call 717-532-3040.

Reach us on the Internet: www.destinyimage.com.

Trade Paper ISBN 978-0-7684-3286-2
Hard Cover ISBN 978-0-7684-3449-1
Large Print ISBN 978-0-7684-3450-7
Ebook ISBN   978-0-7684-9079-4

For Worldwide Distribution, Printed in the U.S.A.

1 2 3 4 5 6 7 8 9 10 11 / 13 12 11 10

Acknowledgments

Every person is a part of all the people they have met. My life was shaped by countless people, most of whom were related to me in church life. It started when I was a senior in high school and continues to the present.

God has great kids, and I have had the privilege of knowing some of His choicest ones. It would be impossible for me to list all the people in whom I have seen and enjoyed the presence of Christ. He has looked so good shining out through their lives for me to enjoy. Even to name all of the churches where I have touched His life and been touched by Him would be a long list. I thank all of you for being vessels displaying the treasure of His life.

Jane and Jesus are so intertwined in my life it is hard for me to tell the difference at times. That is primarily because He lives so conspicuously through her. Of all the great Christians I have met around the world, none has a more consistent walk with Him than the dear person He gave me as a wife 54 years ago. Thank you for showing me Jesus as He is today.

Some people have been up close and indispensable during this past year. Gary and Janell Reutzel, Tom and Jeannie Blanton, Steve and Jean Chapman, and Bud and Liz Starnes have all played key roles in encouraging and lifting Jane and me to a new stage of life.

While writing, I have sought counsel from those who hear from the Lord, who see His big picture, and who notice small typos in the manuscript. I am humbled and grateful for Jack Taylor, Dudley Hall, Bob Roberts, Brian Hook, Dr. R. Michael Siatkowski, Bob Meyer, and Bob Flournoy. Thank you for encouraging me and cheering me on.

I acknowledge that one definition of originality is "the ability to forget where you read it." So many gleanings have come from other people's harvest fields; I may have quotes or thoughts in this book that originated with others. Should that be true, I offer their thoughts again.

Endorsements

The Supernatural Skyline challenges our thoughts and perceptions about the Kingdom of God as a firsthand account of God's work here on earth. From his previous community in West Plains, Missouri, to all over the world, Jim shares inspiring stories of how God's Kingdom is coming here on earth as we faithfully reflect the attitudes and actions of Christ. All who read it will be encouraged, challenged, and motivated to participate in the Kingdom of God!

Dr. Joe White
Founder and President of Men at the Cross
President of Kanakuk Kamps

Pastor Jim Hylton has been an example of spiritual integrity and passion for decades. In his book *The Supernatural Skyline*, Jim leads the thirsty believer to living water, explaining carefully how to experience an authentic spiritual awakening and enjoy true intimacy in Christ.

Craig Groeschel
Founding and Senior Pastor of LifeChurch.tv
Author of *It—How Church Leaders Can Get It and Keep It*

Jim Hylton is a man of mission. Those who walk with him recognize his unique calling regarding the Kingdom of God. He has been entrusted by our Father with a perspective on the Kingdom that is rare. His history is one of being sovereignly placed where the Spirit of God is currently working in the Church. He has seen manifestations of the Kingdom that most Christians have not, yet he hungers for the total picture. As he recounts his own story, we hear a man celebrating the past, but eager to embrace the present. His journey and the insights he has gained in it will inspire you. You will find yourself wanting to discard small and neat categories of God and burst into the empowering liberty of the sons of God.

DUDLEY HALL
President of Successful Christian Living Ministries
Author of *Grace Works, Incense And Thunder, Glad To Be Left Behind, Men In Their Own Skin*

Jim Hylton lifts the veil and allows us to begin to understand the Kingdom. This book will disturb you, excite you, and bring you to your knees. We as leaders in the Body of Christ must read these words and ask our King what part we should play in His Kingdom. This is a reminder that we are to be building His Kingdom, not "our" churches. He challenges us to have a vision for our cities, for the world, and for those hurting people just outside the walls of our fortress churches.

KENT HUMPHREYS
Business Leader & Ambassador of Fellowship of
Companies for Christ International, Christ@Work

I enjoyed reading Jim Hylton's book for several reasons. I have known Jim personally for many years and he has had a significant impact on my life. In 1986, he ministered in my Church in

Australia, and we experienced a time of genuine revival. The power of God fell on people; there were healings and salvations. Our Church was packed for a week of nightly meetings, and people came from other churches. Our well was opened that has not run dry.

For me then, to read *The Supernatural Skyline,* which tells a lot of his story, was encouraging, informative, and challenging.

It is challenging because Jim has been gripped by the grand theme of the Kingdom of God. As I have read this book and listened to Jim minister recently, he has stirred my heart with this theme. He has caused me to revisit this central idea in the teaching of Jesus.

Jim causes us to widen our horizons beyond the local church and enter the great enterprise of the Kingdom of God. Here we see the greater purpose of God and are given an expectancy of God regularly breaking into our lives, ministries, and world in new and surprising ways.

Over the years, Jim has experienced outbreaks of the Kingdom in his ministry. He has seen demonstrations of power, healing, and renewal. His book is a road map for those who want to minister in the power and style of the Kingdom.

I consider it a privilege to recommend *The Supernatural Skyline.*

REV. BARRY MANUEL
Senior Pastor (1982-2009)
Morphett Vale Baptist Church
Adelaide, Australia

Just hearing Jim Hylton preach the first time was enough to impact my life. Even now I remember the heavy presence of God that accompanied that message in Palestine, Texas, as he shared some of the content of this book. Jim is a father, well trained in the Kingdom of God, who from the abundant treasure of his heart will delight you with things new and things old. The message of this book will revolutionize your thinking.

DR. JUAN CARLOS MANZEWITSCH
Leader of "One Prayer, One Mexico"
with up to 85,000 in cities across Mexico
Ministerios Vision Internacional
Queretaro, Mexico

I've read numerous books on the Kingdom, and I believe this is one of the best. Jim asks practical questions and then answers them with wisdom and Kingdom insight in a "down-home style." He teaches us that the Kingdom is more open than we've seen. And as Jim puts it, "A Kingdom expansion in the heart leads to a Kingdom expression in the life." Simply stated, I love this book.

BOB L. PHILLIPS
Senior Pastor of Encourager Church, Houston, Texas
Co-founder of the *Kairos Journal*
Father to the In His Presence Network

America needs something greater than revival. It needs a revolution in which the old order is replaced by a new order—the kingdom of God. Jim Hylton's book will challenge you to see that to the degree Jesus expresses himself, then his kingdom will be manifested in power and practical expressions of love. He urges us, however, to look beyond the transitory blessings associated with revival and to anticipate the transformation that occurs when the King manifests his kingdom in power and practical demonstrations. This is a message America needs.

DR. RICKY PARIS
Vision International, Leader of Churches, Palestine, Texas

Contents

Foreword by Jack Taylor

I approach the task of introducing this volume with deep, varied, and exceedingly intense emotions. I must first address the man, Jim Hylton, and a friendship that spans around 40 years. It is a mistake to separate what a man says or writes from the man himself. I seldom buy a book whose author I know nothing about. A man is inevitably what he says or writes, or at least should be. I do not judge a book by its cover, but by its author. I am impressed, but not moved or changed, by more words chosen with intellect and excellence, strategic arrangement of truth, examples and illustrations, or a combination of all these.

What really excites me is something written or said that has been exemplified in a more profound way than words can express in the life of the one who speaks or writes. I am looking for books that win a place of honor in my library by inviting my repeated attention as I move through the stages of life. I want a book to be an encouragement, a resource, a guide that takes on the sights and sounds of the past and lights the path for the future. I am drawn back again and again to those volumes that have proved durable and relevant through the passing years and changing times.

My friend, Jim Hylton, has written such a book because he is that kind of friend. I am told that there are at least three kinds of friends, all of whom are valuable. First, there are friends for a reason. Perhaps a friendship suddenly appeared in a cataclysmic event, and around that event it was validated and established. Someone was used of God to pull us out of a ditch or stood by us in a dark night. I have had many such friends and will be grateful for them forever. Second, there are friends for a season. Some truth suddenly surfaced between strangers, and that truth became the strong strand that holds lives together. As long as the season lasts, it is vital and throbbing with life, but such friendships as these fade with the coming of new seasons. Third, there are friends for a lifetime. While such friends include the reasons and seasons, the spark that lights the fire of lasting relationship is unmistakable.

Jim Hylton is that kind of friend. We have a friendship that transcends reasons and seasons and, in fact, time itself. We have both moved several times during the years, but when we are together again, it is as if we never left. "In Christ" is a huge place that makes room for friends of all kinds.

Welcome to the world of Jim Hylton and to this unique presentation to which you have addressed yourself. In this book the author dares to address himself to the sacred word in most Christian circles: *revival*. I was intrigued with the originally suggested title: *I Saw the Kingdom Coming and Called it Something Else*. It does make a difference what we call anything. There are as many definitions of revival and many people who study the subject. The histories of nations have been powerfully punctuated and penetrated by seasons and events of God's undeniable manifest presence.

In this volume, Jim has not questioned the value of revival, but instead gives personal testimony of several encounters of such in his own life, church, and region. The telling of the stories throbs with life. They are valid and vital. The uniqueness of this book is that in it we are called to consider that what we called revival or awakening just might be more than the names imply. A recent encounter with the Kingdom of God in the author's life, combined with the burning memories of past encounters with God's presence, has ignited and now fuels the fire of spiritual revitalization that could well release revelations and demonstrations of something that transcends our concepts of regional events. Too many revivals have been similar to a fever followed by a chill, an event that, for a while, was vital and undeniable, but was too-soon lost or dimmed. Some such events even left debris to be carried away.

I cannot forget the time when Jim began to share this concept that involved examining revival in the light of the concept of the Kingdom of God. I saw the value of it almost instantaneously. The Kingdom of God is everything, not a part of something else. It fits nothing, but everything of value fits into it. Everything of value takes on new meaning and durability within the context of the Kingdom of God. The Kingdom track gives direction and definition to revival and grants coherent sustainability.

The Kingdom is forever, revival is for a season. Its inability to endure is not a weakness but a result of the nature of what it brings with it, namely, a fresh sense of God, who has been there all the time: omniscient, omnipresent, omnipotent.

Revival is not a place to settle, but a means of going, a kind of "first step" in what is intended to be a long and fruitful journey. The Kingdom of God puts revival or awakening in its proper context and gives it continuing definition, direction, and dynamics. A spiritual awakening that does not find the Kingdom and the King as its fundamental reason for being will likely begin to be consumed by its own publicity and personality. We are enjoined to pray *"Your Kingdom come, Your will be done..."* (Matt. 6:10). This prayer was given to us from Heaven and is absolutely loaded with the expectation of an affirmative answer. God has given us a mandate to pray the conditions of Heaven down to earth.

This book stands to change the attitude of the Christian world on the very important subject of revival in the classic, historical sense by factoring in the coming of the Kingdom, which gives a move of God's power to sustain itself and spread under the template of God's blessed rule. Is there validity in calling and perceiving revival as the coming of the Kingdom of God? My answer is emphatically, *"Yes!"* In my opinion, no volume in history, recent or ancient, sheds more light on this strategic subject than this treatise you hold in your hand.

JACK TAYLOR, PRESIDENT
Dimensions Ministries
Melbourne, Florida

Foreword by Bob Roberts Jr.

The world is in the midst of a mighty and massive move of God today—but not in the United States. If we are going to see God move here, we are going to have to get in line with His agenda and picture, which means getting in line with the Church globally. It all starts and finishes on "the Kingdom of God" being at hand. What does that look like? What are the implications for me? What are the implications for my church? These are questions that must be tackled and questions that Jim hits head on in his book.

I remember hearing someone quoting Howard Hendricks on challenging young pastors to stay the path and win the race: "If you want to win the race, the way it's going today, forget speed—just finish it, and you just may." Jim is a man of profound wisdom, insight, discipline, and focus. He has kept in the race and continues to run. I don't think I've ever known anyone as balanced or with the breadth of relationships that he has all across the board—which I love.

Jim writes as a pastor who sees the big picture. He traces what God has done in his life from the early days and movements to where it is today. It's as if he's up above all the action and sees where the river has been flowing and where it's headed. We desperately need men like this today to speak into the Church. God didn't start moving with "us," but far before us and outside of us among others and in other places as well.

When I was a student at Baylor University, I would go and listen to him, Jack Taylor, and Peter Lord. Their message was one of surrender to the lordship of Christ and rest in who He is. As God would move, people would get right with Him. I could sit for hours and listen to those men because there was something genuine about them and unadulterated in their message. As years passed, I heard less from them, but no doubt they impacted my views and ministry. Then one day, Jim showed up at my office. He's been one of the most valuable men in my life in the past two years. He worships with us when he isn't speaking, and is an incredible encourager.

He has seen God's Spirit move in powerful and undeniable ways. I do not believe there is an area more susceptible to categorization, classification, isolation, and tribalization than that of the Holy Spirit. Jim pulls together everyone from McGavran, to J. Sidlow Baxter, to Tozer and Simpson, to Dallas Willard, to Henry Blackaby on how God moves powerfully and miraculously in His Kingdom. We desperately need to give people room to be different and grow in this area. If there ever was need for a "both-and" discussion versus an "either-or" division, that day and time is now.

Jim isn't an arrogant spiritualist, but a humble, Spirit-filled man. The Holy Spirit is not optional equipment for the believer—the whole Body of Christ must have the Holy Spirit just to live the Christian life. Somehow, the Holy Spirit has become tied just to the divine and miraculous and the "holy" part has been left out—which has impacted us all. Even sadder, we've lost the "transformative" part of the Holy Spirit that changes whole communities. The Kingdom begins in us, but doesn't stay there—it flows out wherever we are transforming lives and communities. Jim lives on both sides of that world with the ability to bring them together; we so desperately need that today.

Jim is one of the most avid learners I've ever known. He holds on to what God has taught him. Often, people learn only from people in their tribe or persuasion—but not Jim. When God moves in great power, it will not be because of a new way of doing church but because of an obedient way of responding to God. It will require all of us—and our elders, our statesmen, will be at the core of that. They will not be there because they have grown "great" ministries, but because they have grown great lives.

Jim gets the Kingdom. He sees the big picture and how it all fits together. He has the ability to flow where God is moving without having to define it all or explain it all. Jim isn't afraid of "what others would think," and he isn't afraid of being wrong.

Jim is an elder statesman. Our church plants a lot of churches, and we have Jim come and speak to them often. They are "wowed" by him. Young pastors are hungry for more than technique; they are hungry for the power and presence of God.

I am hungry for a great move of God, where the whole Body of Christ is broken and shaken. I see God moving all over the world—I want to see it happen here. I believe we can see what Jim writes about take place here and now.

BOB ROBERTS JR.
Founder and Pastor of Northwood Church, Keller, TX
Author of *Transformation, Glocalization, Multiplying the Church* and *Real-Time Connections*
www.glocal.net

Introduction

"GOD IS ALIVE," was the bold newspaper headline in the West Plains Daily Quill, West Plains, Missouri.[1] Much of the front page was devoted to a story affecting the city and that region of southern Missouri. That story line included the fact that coffeeshop conversations were primarily about the Lord's visitation in the city.

What had started during services in the First Baptist Church of West Plains, Missouri, had extended across the city. The services ended, but the presence of the Lord increased in both intensity and scope.

From the bull-pen of the county jail to the fashionable homes on the hill overlooking the city, the presence of Christ confronted lives. Several people spent the night in their homes, so aware of His presence that they invited Him into their lives in the pre-dawn hours. It was the dawning of a new day for them, as well as for me as a young pastor.

Students in the local high school became so aware of this visitation from Heaven that they disrupted classes with questions about what was happening, and why? The choral director was a popular teacher whose life had been transformed. Many of his classes became forums for discussions about experiencing Christ's life. A court case was solved involving rival banks in the city, which led the judge to open his life to Christ.

America was birthed in such a visitation of the Lord's presence. A new visitation is needed, and I believe it is in the early stages. I am writing this book to share some firsthand accounts from the pages of yesterday, but primarily to focus on the Lord's agenda for such visits today and tomorrow. New headlines could be forthcoming across America chronicling the more recent visitations from the Lord.

This is a book about what I believe is the current agenda of the Lord. What I previously called *revival* is a smaller agenda than what I currently believe the Lord intends. After going back to re-study and re-think the Scriptures, I have become convinced that Jesus came to create a Kingdom expression rather than *revival* as we have labeled it. The term *revival* is not found in the manual of New Testament truth. If we settle for revival, we will settle for too little. Looking back with a new set of lenses, I am convinced that what I saw across three decades was the Kingdom coming.

There is a major difference between a Kingdom perspective of life and the typical approach we have created with the American version of Christianity. Our emphasis has been on people going to church. The Kingdom offer is for the Kingdom to come where we are. Instead of a building and a campus being the center of activities, Kingdom activities are designed for unlimited locations. There are no off-limits places for where Christ's presence can bring God's love and His value for people.

These accounts are about the supernatural as well as the practical expressions of Christ's life through people today. It is a firsthand report on Kingdom sightings, where the presence of Jesus is demonstrated with the reality, *"The kingdom of heaven is at hand"* (Matt. 4:17).

Heaven and earth meet at the skyline of human needs with demonstrations of God's love and life among us. I invite you to walk with me through experiences from years past as they speak of a journey awaiting everyone willing to accept joint ownership in the Father's business. The Father's business is the business of expressing a Kingdom purpose to transform lives, neighborhoods, cities, and nations.

Chapter 1

THE COMING OF CHRIST—NOW AND THEN

THE GIFT OF SIGHT

Many people have prayed, "Thy Kingdom Come." Some have prayed out of habit and some with urgent desire. This book is about Kingdom happenings. It is written with the anticipation that multiplied sightings of His Kingdom will occur.

Seeing is the greatest benefit of being a Christian. Jesus declared that being born again carries the privilege of seeing the Kingdom. Sight never creates anything, but gives the ability to visually register what already exists or can exist. Perhaps the most wasted gift we possess is our sight. We have eyes, but we don't see. Jesus said both eyes and ears contain senses that go unused (see Mark 8:18). Helen Keller was right that those with sight who have no vision are more unfortunate than those without sight at all.[1]

Sight is taken for granted by most of us who were born with a normal ability to record what confronts us visually. Physical sight is a powerful instrument for a sensory recording of what exists. Spiritual sight is even more powerful because we are not only recording what exists, but even the things that are not yet called into existence. Countless people have lived seeing what is yet to come. God is always pleased to display the future to those who with faith have "eyes to see" (see Eph. 1:18).

My naïve approach to physical sight came to an abrupt halt recently. While on a trip, I realized that I was not seeing road signs and was calling on Jane, my wife, to assist me. Though my glasses prescription was only a few months old, I made my way to my optometrist and dear friend. He flashed the usual letters on the screen before me, but with quite different results than a few months before. I had lost three levels of clarity in my vision. Concerned, he referred me to a specialist.

A HOLE TO FILL

While waiting on the specialist, I read literature in the carefully appointed office complex. Among the several brochures was a description of *a macular hole*. That was a new term to me. From this account, I learned that holes may occur in a part of the retina called the macula. The retina is akin to the film of a camera and is the ocular tissue that receives an image that is transmitted to the brain to result in vision. The macula is the center portion of the retina that resolves the finest pinpoint vision that allows us to read small print and recognize small objects. Thus, a hole in this part of the retina can result in a significant loss of vision. Two common causes are trauma from an accident or aging. At 72 years of age, I was a likely candidate for such a problem. Medical repair of such a hole was included in the carefully worded descriptions; surgery was available. Percentages of sight regained were not favorable, but the hole could be closed and vision stabilized. Most ominous in the account was the rehabilitation required.

Rehab would involve having a gas bubble injected into the eyeball for maximum leverage in restoring the normal anatomy of the retina. This would require keeping the head down for 14 days and nights. Special equipment would be available as an extension to the bed. Sleeping face down would enable benefits to continue in the night as well as the day. Bathroom visits and eating would be the only exceptions to the face-down posture. As I finished the booklet and was processing the information, I was called into the doctor's special examination room. A very bright light and his own visual skill, aided by instruments, enabled him to look into the back of my retina for the suspected "hole." Sure enough, he found it.

As a noted retinal specialist, whose reputation causes people to drive 150 miles and more for his services, he outlined what I had just read in the waiting room. Fourteen days in a face-down position would be the only hope of a fractional improvement of the problem. Sight might or might not be improved to a greater degree, but the progression would stop and stabilize at that point.

An assistant gave me a date for the surgery. Instructions were offered with ordering processes for the head rest for sleep and for some comfort during the day while sitting in a chair.

Even a mirror was included for seeing people who came to visit or to watch some TV while positioned with face down.

HEALING GOD'S WAY

As a supernaturalist, I believed this deserved a second opinion. Healings were not uncommon in my experience with the Lord. He had healed me before, and I had seen countless people healed, starting in 1966 when Jane's eyes were healed of astigmatism. She was instantly healed when the Lord spoke to her privately about His desire to repair her sight. Though she had complete faith that He would heal her, she was reluctant because others needed healing worse. Nevertheless, she said simply, "I receive what you want me to have." A physical sensation occurred in her eyes, and she took the newly fitted contact lenses from her eyes and saw with normal vision.

As a busy young pastor, I returned from a personnel committee meeting and drove into our driveway. Something was different as I parked the car under the carport at the home furnished by the First Baptist Church of West Plains, Missouri. The difference was an overwhelming sense of the presence of the Lord that permeated the driveway and carport leading into the kitchen. There in the kitchen I saw Jane at the sink preparing some vegetables, but found the manifest presence of the Lord even stronger. "What is going on here?" was my response. She turned, with the glow of God's presence on her face and with eyes shining, as if they had been washed in some special cleanser.

"The Lord has healed my eyes!" was her joyful reply. I stood there, shocked. I was shocked that He would do that and not consult me. Further, I was trained to disbelieve such accounts. So I responded out of my skills in unbelief, "How do you know?"

With a puzzled look, she used those eyes touched by the Lord to study my face and saw doubt, not faith. Had more time elapsed, she would have seen more in my reasoning process. There was immediately the insecurity of knowing things were not normal and might never be normal again.

Calmly she said, "Let me show you." A skilled seamstress, she took a needle and a thread. With one simple motion, she slipped the thread through the small opening in the needle. I was impressed, to say the least. I wanted to be pleased, but instead of rejoicing, I offered this caution, "Don't tell anyone until we can confirm it with the optometrist. Now, don't tell anyone!"

Although a new walk with the Lord in Spirit-filled living had begun for both of us several weeks before Jane's healing, it took me a few days to adjust my thinking concerning the Lord healing her eyes. The optometrist confirmed that she had 20/20 vision. I asked her to share with the church the blessing of improved sight. Out of that experience, I knew the Lord can still give sight to the blind or improved sight to the impaired.

Therefore, with anticipation, I raised my antennas of faith and expectancy for my eye to be healed supernaturally. I spoke with the Lord about it. There was no clear word from Him. I asked friends who have faith for the supernatural to pray for me. Several times over the next few weeks, I was anointed with oil and prayed for. In Lakeland, Florida, reports of many healings began to surface. A pastor friend from Adelaide, Australia, flew there and gave me a firsthand account of God's presence and power being unfurled. Armed with a sense of expectancy and an invitation from a long-time friend in Florida, I flew there to see if that was to be the venue the Lord wanted to use in healing my eye.

Like the waves in the ocean, waves of God's activity flow in and out in days of His visitation. That was true in Lakeland, and the night I was there the waves were receding, not coming in. It was like the Lord was off duty that night.

I returned home with the words of a friend being replayed in my mind. For years she has been an intercessor for me. While I was her pastor, she took this mantle and faithfully wore it. As I left that pastorate for another, she continued praying for me. She and her husband were part of a prayer group that prayed for my healing. Afterward, she said words that carried a prophetic edge, "This surgery and 14 days face down will be really important in your life." Those were the words being replayed in my mind. They were indeed prophetic.

FACE DOWN, BUT LOOKING UP

Surgery was performed, followed by 14 days of face-down reflection. They were days in which physical sight was limited, but spiritual sight increased. With my face down, few visitors, and limited activity, I had much time to think, retrace my life, and pray for guidance for the running of the race yet ahead.

Suddenly, I considered something that I had never questioned. What if experiences I had called *revival* or *spiritual awakening* for years were an enactment of the Kingdom, and I was calling it something else? My mind reeled under the weighty possibility that I was seeing one thing and calling it by another name. Unlimited time was mine to relive those visitations of God. Many of them I saw firsthand. Others were reported by witnesses and some in books. Within a few days, I concluded that I was seeing Jesus in action. His activity brought Kingdom enactments. I had seen the Kingdom coming, but called it something else.

For me, this was a monumental possibility. I had been identified in the latter part of the 1980s and early 1990s as a man who had seen more "revival" or "spiritual awakening" than any man living in America.[2] That may or may not have been true. Duties were so engaging in those days, I never had time to dwell on those assessments. But it is safe to say I saw the unfurled glory and presence of God in many settings.

With reverence for what I saw and treasured, I began weighing many issues on the scales of my understanding and perception. Revival or enactments from God had occurred. It was supernatural and had very personal and practical benefits. God would show up. When He did manifest His presence, He would set His own agenda and act in keeping with His own character. In none of those many settings did we as leaders determine the expressions of the Lord's visitation. We were not coaching Him. He was coaching us to enter a new engagement of His life and power.

These visits from God had come to others as well. In fact, my own life was shaped both in preparation and participation by those who had seen "genuine revival" and reported it faithfully. I was at the very least a second-generation beneficiary of the greatest engagement of God in "revival history."

Those engagements of God's presence in history are countless. Each visitation affirms that Jesus Christ is the same yesterday, today, and forever. His activities were always in keeping with His sovereign reign as King of kings and Lord of lords. Jesus Christ will always act like Himself. Our expectations of how He should act may not fit His appearances. Long-awaited expectations of His life as Messiah had so crystallized people's thoughts that He broke almost all of those crusted molds. Accommodations of traditions and expectations will not alter His life being manifested. He will be true to Himself. From yesterday through today and forever He will be the "I am" instead of our "oughta be."

AFFECTED BY HIS VISITATION IN CHINA

Perhaps the greatest expression of the Lord's life and presence historically was in China in the late 1920s. Just ahead of Mao Tse-tung's communistic revolution, God touched down in the northern province of Shantung. A lengthy shadow of that appearance of the Lord in northern China stretched across the miles and decades to fall across my life in West Plains, Missouri. God's visitation in our home and the healing of Jane's eyes, as shared earlier, was influenced by that historic enactment of His manifest presence.

Two Norwegian missionaries, Ruth Paxson and Marie Munson, met the Southern Baptist Missionaries in northern China with two questions. "Have you been born again?" and if the answer was in the affirmative, "Have you been filled with the Holy Spirit?" Most missionaries from their denomination would not have been expected to deal with such basic issues. But these were missionaries who had experienced a deep encounter with the risen Lord Jesus.

They were excited to announce that God was going to send "revival" to China and that it would start with the Baptists. When asked, "Why the Baptists?" their answer was simply that Baptists were a people of the Bible who would honor the basic foundations of Scripture.

Revival to them was the ultimate in God's visitation. And their prediction of "revival is coming" was validated with a mighty expression of His life and power.

It was a time of political turbulence in China. Seeds for Mao's revolution were already sown. On more than one occasion, missionaries were advised to leave their stations and stay in a port city ready for evacuation. In one such period, the Baptist missionaries were awaiting possible evacuation. One of the missionary couples was already planning to return to the states.

Dr. C.L. Culpepper was the president of the seminary for Southern Baptists in China. His wife, Ola, had developed an eye problem that was incurable as diagnosed by the Rockefeller Medical Center in Shanghai. Medical reports indicated she would soon be blind. With regret, they felt it wise to go home to the support of family and friends in Texas.

Bertha Smith, a teaching missionary, was very well versed in Scripture and committed to prayer. At her urging, the missionaries met to pray for Ola Culpepper's eyes. During that time, Bertha Smith began to confess her own judgmental attitudes toward some of the missionaries. Others joined in the confessions and requests for forgiveness. Then they prayed for Mrs. Culpepper's eyes to be healed.

This prayer time was attended by the powerful presence of the Lord. Chinese cooks, who served the missionaries, were very impacted as they witnessed these leaders confessing their sins and restoring fellowship with each other. In the atmosphere created by the Lord's strong presence, they experienced Christ for the first time living in them.

As the missionaries rejoiced that the cooks had experienced Christ's life for the first time, they remembered they were praying for Mrs. Culpepper's eyes to be healed. Turning to her, they learned her eyes were healed immediately during that time of prayer.

Those stories and countless others were shared with me by Dr. Jeannette Bealle, a medical doctor serving as a missionary in China with this band of transformed servants. She was part of that prayer meeting when Mrs. Culpepper was healed. Later, having developed tuberculosis, she too was healed as a Chinese pastor prayed quickly and quietly for her. I was honored to serve as Dr. Bealle's pastor in West Plains. When the Lord visited us there, she was quick to announce, "This is like the experiences we had in China."

These catalysts for "revival" became my acquaintances and my heroes. They were people who enjoyed knowing Christ as their Lord and Savior, but also enjoyed knowing Him intimately. He had saved them by His substitution for them in death. Further, they learned He would save them *by His life* being lived out in them. For the first time in my life I learned of the *saving life of Christ* (see Rom. 5:10).

THE LENGTHENED SHADOW OF CHRIST'S LIFE

A lengthened shadow of Christ's life on this earth again fell from as far away as China and as long ago as 1930. He appeared there before I was born in 1935, but He showed himself to me in West Plains. For Dr. Bealle, He was doing it again. For me, it was a first-time encounter with this level of awareness. It was not the first time Jesus was real to me. He was real when I met Him initially as a 16-year-old.

From the time I was nine years old, the Lord had made me aware of my need of Him. At nine I knew Christ had died for me and I deliberately resisted Him. That awareness of His wooing presence greeted me often. As a junior in High School, I took time to read a tract by John R. Rice on "How to be Saved." With my mind made up to welcome Christ in my life, I attended special services at Norwood Baptist Church the next night. When the invitation was given, the same battle over who would rule my life started. Then I decided and stepped out. A peace never known before filled my life as I walked forward. Christ had entered my life and brought to me *"peace with God"* (Rom. 5:1). Christ was immediately real to me, and the next day at school I told everyone who would listen how He had entered my life the night before.

While still a senior in high school and with a call from the Lord, I was asked to pastor a dying church that had nothing to lose. As time went on God became less and less real to me. My years of college training followed, during which I ceased to see Him clearly and depended more and more on my own abilities and developing skills. Yet my heart became more and more hungry and at times desperate to know Him better. Going to West Plains was an answer to the cry of my heart to know the Christ who I saw in Colossians. As a very young pastor, I was straining to see through the dark smoky glass. To my amazement, I saw that *"Christ in you"* is the hope of glory (Col. 1:27). Indeed He was in me, but the glory was not evidenced except on rare occasions.

Yet, my favorite phrase in Scripture, "and suddenly" was about to happen. "And suddenly," there He was standing clearly in my consciousness. This time, He was more real than when I was 16. At 30, I was seeing Him in a way I had never seen Him. He came showing me His love. He came showing me the value He gives to all people. He came showing me the false motives of my life. He came showing me out of Colossians that I was complete in Him. He came showing me that He was in me. This Christ, so remarkably declared in Colossians, was in me. Christ in me was the hope of glory, and His attending glory was being declared.

GLORY WITHOUT BOUNDARIES

This glory engagement permeated the First Baptist Church worship center, where I was pastoring at that time. Months before we had entered a beautifully crafted and decorated building complete with a phone at my seat on the platform. I could call the ushers, the sound technicians, and even the offices, if people were stationed there. One station was sadly missing. I could not call the throne room of God. This "and suddenly" included a reconnection with Heaven. Our building was beautifully decorated, but it was quickly redecorated with the "Glory of God." God's presence was declared, and countless people were overwhelmed by this invasion of our privacy.

Glory knows no boundaries. What that auditorium contained spread on to the town square two blocks away. There at the center of the square was the courthouse. The top floor was the county jail. I had never made calls there. I was only calling on people who would continue to fill our much larger building.

Christ's life in me was compelling me to go to the jail. I did, and found it packed with men who had escaped from a Washington state penitentiary. The sheriff assembled them. With complete honesty I told them I had never done a jail service and knew nothing about how to do it, but I knew a jail-house story. I read to them the Paul and Silas experience in the Philippian jail out of Acts chapter 16. Then I shared with them the question of the jailer, *"What must I do to be saved?"* (Acts 16:30). I told them the answer Paul gave, *"Believe on the Lord Jesus Christ and you will be saved and your household"* (Acts 16:31). I knelt in prayer. I heard the thud of knees hitting the concrete floor. I prayed, and they prayed aloud after me.

When I looked up only one man had not kneeled, but he was very impacted. Most were weeping openly, unashamedly. There Jesus was again. This time, Jesus was real in a jail. He was as much at home there in the county jail as in the church building.

Later, He would make His way down into the judge's chambers to reach the heart of the circuit judge who was not a Christian. The judge was presiding over a court case that was a "hot potato." Two banks were litigating a disputed property. The issue was more about power than profit, or even justice. One of the banks was represented by attorneys in our church. The other bank had a major shareholder who was also a member, so the issue carried into the church.

As the Lord made His presence known around our town, the attorneys turned their lives and practice over to Him. He took them at their word. They prayed for a resolution of that case. The opposing bank's largest shareholder was so moved by the Lord's presence in our church that he called me. He said, "I want to offer that property in dispute to be purchased by the First National Bank." First National had tried repeatedly to purchase the disputed property. He quickly added the stipulation that they could choose to pay whatever they determined, but with the understanding it would be given to the church and the Lord's cause.

The offer was taken by the attorneys to the president of First National Bank, and they asked me to accompany them. They asked me to explain why the offer was made. There Jesus was again, this time in the home of the wealthiest man in town, solving a court case.

When the judge knew the Lord had attended the county jail and had met with people of power and wealth in the solving of that case, he opened his life to Christ. One of the attorneys led him to the Lord. There Jesus was again, this time entering the chambers of the heart of a judge who sat in the chambers of the court.

This glory rolled on across the city and into the lives of countless people who came into the city. Some came to see for themselves. Others were driving around the bypass of highway 63 and were overwhelmed by His presence and sensed an urgency to drive into the city. From that city His presence spread consciously to other cities.

HIS KINGDOM BY ANY OTHER NAME IS STILL HIS KINGDOM

Now, years later, I am looking at that transforming event in my life and wondering if I gave that manifestation a name that was not the best description of what He was doing. It was His doing, and He had the right to give it a proper name. Perhaps, it is not too late to name it properly. At any rate I am asking you to walk with me from that event to others and consider the possibility that we are anticipating "revival" or God "doing it again" when He is seeking to give us far more than what we are asking for. It is my carefully considered conclusion that we are asking for a "narrow-cast" and He is offering a "broad-cast."

His coming to us in West Plains was a declaration and demonstration of His glory. That appearance is described in Psalm 24:7: *"Lift up your heads, O you gates! And be lifted up, you everlasting doors! And the King of glory shall come in."*

The "King of Glory" had come. A king cannot come without bringing His Kingdom. We had become gates and doors permitting Him access. He came and went as He chose. With His coming as King of glory, His kingdom was enacted. This was His own description of His coming to His people, *"The kingdom of heaven is at hand"* (Matt. 4:17). With Him was the Kingdom enacted—at hand. I was seeing the Kingdom because I was seeing the King of Glory. Jesus had become real to me. His Kingdom was just as real. But I was perhaps not ready to understand what I saw. Or was I simply accommodating terms that had been handed to me as traditions?

The coming of Jesus in manifested presence is ever occurring. John described it this way: *"We beheld His glory, the glory of the only begotten of the Father full of grace and truth"* (John 1:14). Jesus does not come leaving His glory behind. Glory is a continuous accompaniment of His life, though not everyone will see it. His Kingdom is ever accompanying Him as well. It would be impossible for the King to be present and His

Kingdom not be part of His presence. Thus, the manifest presence of Jesus is also the manifest presence of His life in action.

My own definition of the Kingdom is simply, "Jesus in action." That enacting presence may take on varying scales and degrees. His action may take place through people or apart from people. When He decided to visit Saul of Tarsus, He showed up to speak for Himself. (see Acts 9:5). No doubt He appeared to Saul through Stephen's witness of "seeing Jesus" as he was beaten to death. (see Acts 7:55-56). But when He readied His entry in Saul's life, He appeared to him personally, with the question, *"Saul, Saul why do you persecute me?"* Saul did not know who He was, but knew His title, *"Who are you, Lord?"* Then He received the clear disclosure, *"I am Jesus, whom you persecute."* Many today know His name, but do not know His title, *Lord*. Later, He came and spoke through others to Saul.

THE CHURCH WITH A HOLE IN THE EYE

We are not whole when we have a hole in the eye. Age was the reason for my hole in the eye. The aging Church has also developed a macular hole. That is why a new generation of leaders is planting new churches instead of trying to repair the systems already in place. We are not seeing clearly.

Before the macular hole in my eye was successfully closed, I would close my other eye and whatever I saw would be greatly reduced in size. A person's face would pull inward and all but disappear. Letters would pull into a small indistinguishable bundle. Much of current Church life is like that. Our macular hole is causing important things to disappear or become muddled. Our vision is often limited to ourselves and to our cause. Self-consciousness eclipses a Christ-consciousness and obscures a Kingdom-awareness.

Jesus is still standing at the door of the Church and lovingly knocking to gain admission. Just as my hole in the eye was repaired surgically, the hole in the eye of the Church can be repaired when we allow the Lord to touch our eyes.

Doors that were closed to Him in the past were opened and He stepped in. When He comes, the Kingdom comes. He taught us to pray, *"Thy kingdom come."* Perhaps we have prayed those words more from memory than a hunger for Him to come. But He takes us seriously, and He comes, bringing His Kingdom engagement with Him.

This book is about His Kingdom coming. It is a firsthand account of such activities with conclusions that come from a Kingdom encounter. I have a renewed excitement in me to see His Kingdom coming. May this book serve as part of His known will to answer the prayer He instructed us to pray, *"Thy kingdom come."*

Chapter 2

THE SHAKING OF AWAKENING—BUT FOR WHAT?

For many, the initial waking from sleep is often an intrusion into a preferred state. Wakefulness has interrupted unconsciousness. Consciousness is the goal of wakefulness. To wake up in a stupor is counterproductive. Waking up to the offers of a new day, to the people we know and love, and to the presence of God with us is reason for consciousness.

God is committed to awaking His people.

> *And do this, knowing the time, that now it is high time to awake out of sleep; for now is our salvation nearer than when we first believed. The night is far spent, the day is at hand; let us, therefore, cast off the works of darkness,*

and let us put on the armor of light (Romans 13:11-12).

There is more to see, more to experience, and more to engage in than we are aware of. God is taking steps to awaken us.

Sleepwalking is scary and even dangerous. My college roommate was a sleepwalker. With eyes open and his brain turned off, he would get up and walk through the room. He could even carry on limited conversation in that state of unconscious autopilot. An emergency room doctor friend of mine would pull long hours of duty at the hospital. He warned the nurses to be sure he was awake because he could answer the phone and give prescriptions while asleep.

Most frightening is the sleepwalking Church. We act for the most part like we are awake, but our level of consciousness is so limited that we are actually asleep. Like my doctor friend, we even give prescriptions for people's needs without full consciousness. Our prescriptions leave people with little or no help and sometimes are even harmful.

GOD SPEAKS AND EVEN SHAKES US TO AWAKEN US

God's usual method of waking us is to speak. *"And God said"* was the creative crescendo that brought everything into being that now exists (see Gen. 1:3,6,9,14,20,24,26). God said, and whatever He said became what He declared it to be.

"Hath God said?" is the questioning that leads to the perversion and corruption of God's creative order (Gen. 3:1 KJV). God creates. Satan corrupts. The first corruption came when

satan raised the question with Adam and Eve, "Hath God said?" They paused to entertain that possibility and bought the lie to follow appealing suggestions.

Each time God speaks, He is either creating or shaking from satan's grasp His corrupted creation. His voice awakens us when we are light sleepers. When we do not respond, God may add to the speaking a required shaking to arouse us from sleep.

> *See to it that you do not refuse Him who speaks. If they did not escape when they refused Him who warned them on earth, how much less will we, if we turn away from Him who warns us from heaven? At that time His voice shook the earth, but now He has promised, "Once more I will shake not only the earth but also the heavens." The words "once more" indicate the removing of what can be shaken—that is, created things—so that what cannot be shaken may remain. Therefore, since we are receiving a kingdom that cannot be shaken, let us be thankful, and so worship God acceptably with reverence and awe, for our* **"God is a consuming fire"** *(Hebrews 12:25-29 NIV).*

If God shakes the heavens, which are designed to manifest Him, and likewise shakes the earth, designed to show His workmanship, shouldn't we expect Him to shake the Church as well? An awakened Church may be a shaken Church.

Why is God so insistent about awakening us? Is awakening a mere cosmetic application to make us look good? Is it a wave of new excitement that blows as a fresh wind to drive out the smog of dullness? Is it a new truce to prevent opposing forces from destroying each other with gossip or slander?

God speaks for Himself:

> *How shall we escape [appropriate retribution] if we neglect and refuse to pay attention to such a great salvation [as is now offered to us, letting it drift past us forever]? For it was declared at first by the Lord [Himself], and it was confirmed to us and proved to be real and genuine by those who personally heard [Him speak]. [Besides this evidence] it was also established and plainly endorsed by God, who showed His approval of it by signs and wonders and various miraculous manifestations of [His] power and by imparting the gifts of the Holy Spirit [to the believers] according to His own will* (Hebrews 2:3-4 AMP).

When God speaks, shaking results in signs and wonders of miraculous manifestations of His presence in the Church. A sleepwalking Church that awakens will leave the complacent status quo and take on the look and life of God Himself. *"Let us therefore, receiving a kingdom that is firm and stable and cannot be shaken, offer to God pleasing service and acceptable worship with modesty and pious care and godly fear and awe"* (Heb. 12:28 AMP).

God is like a parent who is wide awake and eagerly waiting for His child to wake up to enjoy the day with Him. He awakens us to get us in on what He has already arranged to share with us. God is shaking us to a new level of consciousness. What does He want us to see? What does He have for us to be part of?

My conclusion is that the awaited awakening is a far bigger agenda than simply awakening the Church to what the Church was engaged in before sleep came. God is eager to introduce us to more than simply "successful Church life." A Kingdom perspective extends far beyond the boundaries of Church life as we currently know it. Church life will not be stifled or diminished by awakening to the Kingdom. In fact, the Church will function in the power and blessing of the Lord. The early Church was awake. It was reported by those still partially asleep that the world was turned upside down (see Acts 17:6). Actually, a world order was turned right side up. Right side up is a Kingdom-ordered world being governed by the presence of Jesus.

The wide world of Kingdom awareness awaits us as we awaken. Trying to compress the Kingdom into Church life as we now know it would be like trying to compress a sprawling, 50-square-mile city into a one-half-square-mile village. Our vision is too small and our agenda is too limited. We are to awaken to something bigger than revival and self-consciousness. Our awakening to Christ the King and the Kingdom, His life in action, is God's goal.

Chapter 3

RECOVERING THE BLUEPRINTS OF THE KINGDOM

Controversy accompanied the development of the Dallas–Fort Worth Airport. Most of that controversy had to do with its location and why it was not built closer to Dallas, the larger of the two cities it served. Most theories credited Amon Carter with the influence for its location. It was said that his influence came from buying ink by the barrel for printing *The Fort Worth Star Telegram* and amassing piles of money printed by the U.S. Treasury Department. With that leverage, he supposedly pushed the airport closer to Fort Worth rather than where the larger city of Dallas desired it to be.

Then I learned the truth from a man who became a close friend. He was part of the planning group selected by the

Federal Aviation Authority to plan and develop the airport. When I asked him why the busy airport was located where it is, his reply was simply, "We let a computer tell us where to put it!" Then he added that all the data they could amass from land available to population projections, elevations, existing flight patterns, and residential areas near possible sites were programmed into a computer. The decision was made when a computer voted. There were no opposing votes.

His most amazing experience with DFW was yet to come. After retiring from the FAA, he continued as a consultant to the airport board. Years went by and airport traffic increased to a level that expansion of the airport was necessary. Again he was called in.

Several new runways were needed and being designed. He shared with the planning group that master planning had anticipated all the expansion that would ever be needed. When he asked to see a copy of the master plans, an embarrassed official acknowledged that they had gone through all of their archives and could not locate a master plan for DFW Airport.

Knowing his pack-rat habit of keeping everything of importance, even to the point of building a storage area in his backyard, he thought he just might know where a set existed. Sure enough, in the attic of his home in Manitou Springs, Colorado, he found a copy of the original master plan.

Armed with the plans, he met with the committee and shared with them what was envisioned in the initial layout. Future expansion was already planned for.

When he shared the story with me, I realized that we have done the same thing with the master plan for the Kingdom expansion. Buried in the attic of Church life is a plan that calls for expansion with a comprehensive overlay for life. Nothing is overlooked because *"His divine power has given to us all things that pertain to life and godliness, through the knowledge of Him"* (2 Pet. 1:3 NKJV).

Verses 10-11 point out that, by following His blueprint, *"you shall never fall: For so an entrance shall be ministered unto you abundantly into the everlasting kingdom of our Lord and Saviour Jesus Christ"* (2 Pet. 1:10-11 KJV).

LOSING THE BLUEPRINTS

I still find it hard to believe my friend's account of such high-level mismanagement. Knowing his reputation for total honesty and his character, I know it happened. More amazing is how we could have neglected to consult the blueprints left to us as the Church. Our mismanagement is even more incongruous.

A pastor who found the blueprints of the Kingdom, and has done as much as anyone I know to get the expansion going, offers an explanation for our incompetency.

Dr. Bob Roberts is pastor of Northwood Church in North Fort Worth, Texas. Their expansion of the Kingdom includes over 125 churches planted in a 20-year span. These churches include local, national, and international start-ups. Several countries are being impacted through their influence and presence in key cities. His knowledge of the master plan sees nations and cities as being important in Kingdom values, not just church life and activities.

With clarity based on years of studying the blueprints and years of experience in growing up in church life, Bob Roberts states that we have gone to the wrong end of the Gospel drawings to know what to do. He concludes that we have gone to the end of Matthew's account of the life of Jesus to the Great Commission, *"Go therefore and make disciples of all nations..."* (Matt. 28:19). If we had started where Jesus started, we would have gone to the first part of Matthew and worked forward. In that forward review, we would have heard Jesus instruct us to *"Seek first the kingdom of God and His righteousness, and all these things shall be added to you"* (Matt. 6:33). This insightful pastor is saying that, had we checked the fine print, we would have heard Jesus further instruct us to pray, *"Your kingdom come. Your will be done on earth as it is in heaven"* (Matt. 6:10). Checking the "fine print" means not small print, but the rest of the print. Everything God has put in print is "fine," and we need to read what He has said again.

Nowhere does Jesus suggest that we should be praying, "Your church be built," but instead, *"Your kingdom come."* In fact, when Jesus did introduce the Church much later on, He indicated that He would build it (see Matt. 16:18). Our focus was always to be on the Kingdom. Seeking first the Kingdom carries the serendipity of everything else being added that is needed. We seek the Kingdom. He builds His Church.

What Bob Roberts has lived out is not a theory, but an experience. He has had a Kingdom focus with Kingdom engagement, and Jesus has built the Church. By focusing on the Church seeking to fulfill a "great commission," there has instead been "a great omission." We have omitted what Jesus made the centerpiece of His life and ministry—namely, His Kingdom.

He announced, *"The kingdom is at hand"* (Matt. 4:17). We have announced "the Church is at hand." Or we have said to the Church, "revival is at hand" or "awakening is at hand." His Kingdom was His enactment. With His presence came His actions, which are Kingdom reality.

No one that I know has a clearer understanding of the disconnect between Kingdom values and methods and our attempt to evangelize the world than Bob Roberts. With clarity of vision and keen perception, he cuts through issues and gets to the heart of Kingdom implications:

> We have to move from a one-shot evangelism perspective that says, "Boom—here's the four spiritual laws. If you don't accept them, it's over. I've done my duty" to a radically different faith response where one is unabashedly proclaiming the gospel, and serving, and loving.
>
> The kingdom is a wholistic, viral response to different infrastructures of society within a connected world. Today, with all the connections of globalization and the various domains of the world intersecting our lives, it's easier than ever to practice kingdom work because the kingdom itself is a viral, organic response. It's societal, as opposed to religious, skeletal, or institutional.[1]

That does not mean he has no appreciation for the Church. To the contrary, he loves the Church and does a superb job leading Northwood. It is his love for Christ that gives him a love for missions, but missions is not about building the

Church, but building the Kingdom. He teaches the family of God at Northwood that "they do not do missions; they are the mission." Wherever they are, they are on mission, starting at home with good family relationships, at work with good work ethics, in their neighborhoods, in their cities, and on to the nations of the world.

He describes the early Church:

> The early church accomplished the spread of the gospel through leveraging the existing cultural and societal infrastructures for its own purposes. "Christianity's rapid growth could not have taken place without the empire's expansive urban infrastructure."
>
> In contrast, today "church" has become the focus separating Sunday from society, and the result is devastating. We give far more attention to the "Sunday event" or "show" to fill seats than we do anything else. We have the wrong measurement tools. Monday is a better measurement—no, Thursday (get farther away from Sunday)—than anything. The kingdom does not measure church but rather in examples like society, at work, at play, and with family. This is what people are discovering and, sadly without pastors and churches.[2]

To fail to see the value of the Church would be like wanting to bulldoze all of the existing miles of runways at DFW before the expansion took place. It is a question of getting the original plan and building or developing from this point on. What was the original plan?

The original plan was allowing Christ's life to create an order of authority and life that is the reenactment of Himself. His presence brings His Kingdom. His power brings His benefits to all who will receive them. There are more Kingdom benefits than we are utilizing. The original blueprints for the expansion must be followed.

From years of seeing these benefits expressed both supernaturally and practically, I am going to share at least a part of what I believe Kingdom life can look like.

Chapter 4

A CHURCH AWAKENS
AT GRACELAND

Elvis Presley named his mansion in Memphis Graceland, but it is an even better name for a church. The greatness of Graceland's name is because God is always offering grace. Jesus came displaying grace and truth. Paul opened every epistle with a salutation of "grace be unto you." God's grace expresses His nature of offering the gracelets of His love.

Graceland Baptist Church, New Albany, Indiana, became the setting for a visitation of God in 1980. God started creation with land or territory. It was not an institution in the sky. It was land or territory to be occupied and ruled by those He made in His image. Whatever life with God is like, it includes land or territory. Church life that connotes land or territory is a better picture of what God designed than attractive buildings where people gather. Graceland was territory awaiting God's occupancy.

A good name is not enough for God to visit. Graceland's name was not the reason God was attracted to that group of people. A good heart attracts the manifest presence of God. People look at the outside. God is looking at the x-rays of the heart (see Acts 15:8). "A person after God's own heart" is the person God likes to hang out with.

HISTORY IS ALWAYS "HIS STORY"

A struggling mission church in New Albany, Indiana, across the Ohio River from Louisville, Kentucky, faced possible disbanding. Sagging attendance, financial shortages, and lack of vision settled like fog from the nearby river. A woman of prayer, Miss Clara Myers, urged them to find a pastor and press on.

Across the river they found a man who had moved to Louisville with his family to attend The Southern Baptist Theological Seminary. As a businessman, Elvis Marcum had heard the call of God to vocational ministry. Though mature in age, he was inexperienced in Church life. He made the first of many courageous decisions to accept their call for him to be pastor at Graceland.

At the seminary he had access to some of the best theological minds in the world. This did not keep this pastor from conferring often with Miss Clara Myers. He combined academic training with practical experience. More importantly, he combined scriptural knowledge with Miss Myers's counsel to depend on the indwelling Holy Spirit's power. Faithfully, he found devotional time with the Lord each day. Often on his knees, he called to the Lord to visit Graceland.

Elvis Marcum was not afraid to dream dreams and then to work untiringly to see them fulfilled. A struggling church became an example of what can happen with the Lord's blessing. Increasing crowds required that they leave the landlocked location they occupied. They purchased and moved to an 80-acre tract of land. Beautiful colonial-style buildings were erected. Athletic fields and facilities were added to house the growing church family. A retreat center with a motel-like structure to house leaders coming for training went up in a wooded area on the back of the property.

A staff with talent, a hunger for God, and a work ethic like the pastor's was in place. They were as prepared for awakening and shaking as any staff could have been.

Elvis was a bold, strong, exciting leader. He was well received, whether giving motivational addresses to insurance companies or preaching at Graceland or churches across America. All the standards of success in people's eyes existed. He shared with me that "all the emptiness of a man's heart wanting God's presence" also accompanied that stage of his life. Outwardly successful and inwardly empty, he did what all genuine men of God eventually do, he cried out to God.

With that heart cry for God to show Himself, he brought men to Graceland to share a message of personal intimacy with God. That list included Peter Lord, Jack Taylor, and Manley Beasley. During the time Manley Beasley shared there, Elvis was personally broken and spent days weeping and sharing with the staff and church his hunger for God to show Himself strong to them.

That was the first tremor of shaking that touched Graceland. Elvis never let up. Daily he sought the Lord. Daily he cried out from his heart in the basement room of his home for God to visit his church, city, and region.

Then, seeming defeat struck. While visiting Fort Worth, Texas, Elvis and Virginia, his beautiful wife, walked to a meeting downtown. On the way, Elvis was stricken with a severe heart attack.

At the very time he was receiving medical care in Harris Hospital, Fort Worth, where I lived, I was in New Albany, Indiana, speaking in an associational meeting on prayer for awakening. Some of those sessions were in the Graceland building. Though I did not know him, when I returned to Fort Worth, I went to see him at the hospital. I found a man weak and sick, but optimistic. We talked of the need for God's power to be manifested. He insisted that I come to Graceland to lead in a week's emphasis on spiritual awakening. His own condition was anything but stable, but his vision for God's visitation was unchanged.

My next open date was not until five months later, May 18, 1980. Reluctantly, I gave him the date. Two things concerned me. Primarily, I worried about his health and the uncertainty of him being able to resume his duties. Secondarily, I wondered whether the time of the year would work, since it was so close to the time of schools closing for summer vacations and people not being free to attend the services.

After four weeks rest in Fort Worth, Elvis and Virginia returned to New Albany. His local doctor advised total rest for six more months. The doctors were not telling him they thought he would never be able to pastor Graceland again, but they communicated that to Virginia. He was already a diabetic, and the heart condition exacerbated his blood sugar level. Early retirement or a move to a small church with fewer duties would be the likely choice.

The man who was the proverbial "candle lit on both ends" was facing six months of rest. The Indiana winter would not be the best place for maximum recovery. Through a friend, a home in Florida was made available to him for the anticipated six-month sabbatical.

Faithful still to his early-morning times with the Lord, Elvis began reading through the Gospel of Mark. He had done exhaustive studies in Mark's Gospel as a seminary student. Though he had written papers from his studies, he was reading this time with eyes of devotion. This was not merely an academic pursuit. He saw and heard Jesus in a new way. Awakening was occurring to him.

Jesus the healer appeared, as if for the first time, on every page in Mark's account. A sick man has no problem being motivated to consider divine healing. He heard the Lord speaking to his own heart, telling him he was being healed. With his usual excitement, he shared the good news with Virginia.

Virginia wanted a healthy husband. Her love for and devotion to Elvis was a model for pastor's wives across the country. Yet, unlike Abraham, who did not stagger at God's promise, she staggered. She staggered because of fear. She knew of pastors who had been healed and had been ostracized by their churches and peers. Later she and Elvis would laugh at her response. Facing a man whose future was very uncertain due to his health, she said, "Elvis, if the Lord heals you, it could ruin your ministry!"

Shaking had occurred in a pastor's wife just as it had occurred in her husband. It's amazing that healing could be viewed as a threat to a very successful ministry. It was not long until she embraced healing for her husband and others with joy instead of misgivings.

A healed pastor returned to Indiana. Doctors confirmed the reality of God's power being released in repairing a damaged heart. The church was grateful that their much-loved leader was restored.

The pastor not only returned much earlier than expected, he returned with a fire and boldness they had never known. Virginia had to adjust to a new man in the pulpit. She was accustomed to a man who was organized, positive, and motivational, a man whose preaching flowed with a predictable polish. Now she listened to a man hitting hard at sin, at issues that matter most, and calling for people to believe God for the supernatural.

This shaking was severe, but she responded favorably and began enjoying the pastor who was obviously hearing from God and sharing what he heard. Preaching can easily become a verbal art form. People attend church like people who walk through art galleries, admiring the skills of the artist. Verbal artistry can leave people with the enjoyment of the art of communication and void of the experience of hearing God's voice. Richard F. Lovelace, professor of Church history at Gordon Conwell Seminary, says of another generation needing a fresh encounter with God: "Many American congregations were in effect paying their ministers to protect them from the real God."[1]

Graceland was hearing a pastor who was hearing God. They were hearing God also and were eager to hear more.

Graceland became a church reaching the "up and out" as well as the "down and out."

May 18 arrived, and on the flight to Graceland that Sunday afternoon, after speaking at Lake Country Baptist Church, I too started hearing from God. Exhausted from two services and the days immediately preceding, I fell asleep on the plane before it left the runway at DFW. I awakened with Psalm 85 flowing through my mind like a fresh mountain stream. I knew it was the word I was to share that night.

Elvis had shared a convicting message that morning, emphasizing that judgment begins at the house of God. That word had convicted and stirred people's hearts all day. On the heels of his word came the message *"Will you not revive us again that your people may rejoice in you. —We will hear what God the Lord will speak, for he will speak peace to his people. —Mercy and truth are met together; righteousness and peace have kissed each other"* (Psalm 85:6,8,10).

Men in spiritual leadership in America had been calling for awakening. In 1979, Billy Graham, the dean of evangelical leaders, had leaned forward with those piercing blue eyes and looked in the eyes of notable leaders and said, "Without revival our republic cannot last another 1,000 days."[2]

That meant that in three years we would not be a nation operating as a republic based on laws our forefathers wrote. Those laws were based on their understanding of God's word. Men such as Dr. D. James Kennedy of Coral Ridge Presbyterian Church, Dr. Bill Bright of Campus Crusade for Christ, Pat Robertson of CBN Broadcasting, and James Robinson, evangelist of Fort Worth, all agreed with that assessment.[3] Each of them began calling for America to return to the Lord in repentance.

Out of that same sense of urgency, I shared that night at Graceland. The first invitation I gave resulted in the seats emptying and the front filling with people. The aisles were also filled with people who fell on their knees before the Lord. A holy awe fell over us. For 30 to 40 minutes, people prayed and surrendered themselves to every part of the Lord they knew.

On the way back to my motel room, not much was said. It seemed too holy a time to even comment. I told Elvis Marcum: "Not since 1966 in the First Baptist Church of West Plains, Missouri, have I seen such a response." Thoughtfully he responded, "In the 17 years I have been pastor here, I have never seen our people so broken before the Lord."

When we assembled on Monday night, it was a typical response of people in Southern Indiana. Only about half of the crowd of the night before gathered in the busy metropolitan area of greater Louisville. Initially I was disappointed, but sensed again the crowding of the Lord's presence. The invitation was visited with strong conviction as people streamed to the front virtually leaving the seats empty. Again, the choir not only led in the singing of praise, but also led in the response to the Lord in the altar. That pattern never varied through the entire 18-week encounter that followed.

The series of services were scheduled to close on Wednesday night. By then it was like trying to stop the cascading waters of Niagara Falls. Who would dare get under the avalanche of power to stop it? We agreed to continue through Friday night, the first of the series of weekly extensions.

By Friday night, the attendance had grown and there was an even greater intensity of the Lord's manifested presence.

With that degree of intensity of the Lord's presence, we determined that we must extend into the second week.

God had filled Graceland with His own life and agenda. We prayed and claimed His continuing presence. With His coming in authoritative presence, we were experiencing the truth that all power and authority belong solely to Him. But He will transfer that authority to others who will humble themselves before Him and receive His operative life. Weeks unfolded as we continued to download from the Lord the things He was leading us in doing.

Soon Elvis Marcum was urging me to share with the people that they could come forward for healing. He had found healing from the Lord and wanted others to experience those benefits. My response was to encourage him to give that invitation. I pointed out that he was the pastor and the one who had recently experienced healing. He wouldn't even consider giving such an invitation.

I told him I had never given an invitation for people to come for healing, though I had seen people healed just sitting in the services hearing the living Word of God. For example, a pastor's wife in Chillicothe, Missouri, had acute asthma and was told by doctors to move to Arizona as her only possible means of prolonging normal life. Sitting and listening to the book of Romans, she felt refreshing air rush into her lungs as if she was taking a breathalyzer. She then realized that her breathing was normal and she had enough breath support to sing.

When I told Elvis I could not give an invitation for healing unless I sensed definite leadership from the Lord, he understood. He simply shared that he would be praying for guidance for me, but would not give an invitation himself.

Three nights later, at the end of the invitation time, I heard myself say, as if I was listening to someone else, "If any of you have issues with poor health, you may come to have the deacons pray for you." I reminded them that the pastor had been healed and that they had the same rights to Christ's life and power. A large number of people came forward. Elvis decided the deacons should anoint with oil on the basis of James 5:13-15. It was a fiasco. They couldn't find any oil and so dispatched a deacon to get cooking oil from the kitchen. This proved appropriate, because the Lord was cooking up something new.

One of the people coming for healing was a tennis coach who had hurt her arm demonstrating how to serve a tennis ball. I was not qualified to identify the problem, but it sounded like she had injured her rotator cuff. She was in a great deal of pain and had not been able to pick up a tennis racket. My inexperience and much of my training in unbelief still guiding my thinking. I concluded the Lord would not heal an injury suffered from stroking a tennis ball. After all, I reasoned, tennis was not a high priority with the Lord; otherwise she would have been born with a tennis racket instead of her hand on the right arm.

She was immediately healed. All of my reasoning was faulty. The Lord knew what He was doing and did it without my understanding.

Not only was she healed, but out of the joy of that experience with the Lord, she went to school the next day telling all of her students to get over to the services and experience the Lord for themselves. Countless students came, and many of them experienced the Lord for the first time or committed their lives to Christ again.

A new part of Graceland was being possessed. An invasion from Heaven was taking territory not yet occupied. Divine healing was occurring, and with it, many questions.

Chapter 5

HEALTH ASSURANCE—A KINGDOM BENEFIT

Awakening always includes awakening to Christ being the same yesterday, today, and forever. The eternal Christ does not go through stages of aging or adaptation to fit our preconceived caricatures of Him. As Christ visited Graceland, He came with the same Kingdom benefits He brought to His own homeland. Kingdom rights are not dispensational or periodic, but they are for now; they are eternal and universal. The wake of His manifest presence in history fully documents that He is the unchanging, unalterable Christ.

Divine healing is a welcome word to the sick, a questionable word to the scientific, and a controversial word to much of the Church today. More question marks than exclamation marks have existed in the evangelical Church concerning healing: "Is healing for today?" "Didn't healing end with the apostles?" "Does God want to heal everyone?" "Isn't sickness part of God's plan for dying?" "Is healing in the atonement as part of salvation?" "What about medicine in the light of divine healing?"

This is not an attempt to answer all these questions. The answers can be found as the Lord speaks His word to those seeking answers.

One size does not fit all when God answers. God offers sizes to fit our backgrounds, our needs, and our understandings. He may also reshape us to a new size.

Some of these questions may be answered in the accounts I am giving. Among those who have searched for God's list of answers are Dr. J. Sidlow Baxter, respected British Baptist, (evangelical) who struggled with seeking to claim healing for himself and then experienced divine healing. He carefully searched the Scriptures to establish a Biblical basis for the Church awakening to this neglected ministry. His conclusion is solid,

> Although much present-day preaching on divine healing is, in my judgment, mis-founded on wrong interpretation of scripture, there remains nevertheless sufficient evidence in the New Testament that a ministry of divine healing for the body is meant to be still in operation today, at least inside local Christian churches. As we have seen, there is (1) clear promise of such healing in response to faith, (2) a clear inclusion of healing in the Spirit's distribution of "gifts" among

believers, (3) clear reference to such healing as being experienced by the Lord's people in those early days of the church. Therefore we should guard against letting hostile reactions against off-center extremists blind us to the true teaching of the word. Prejudice is sometimes even worse than extremism! Yes, divine healings are meant for the church today.[1]

Another internationally known seeker of truth was Dr. Donald A. McGavran, dean emeritus and former senior professor of missions, church growth, and South Asian studies at the School of World Mission, Fuller Theological Seminary in Pasadena, California. He believed we would be wise to rethink the issue of divine healing.

These quotes are from an address he gave to the Christian and Missionary Alliance missionaries in Lincoln Nebraska in 1979:

Christians have a problem in the Western society. The sciences war with their Christian faith. Divine healing was an essential part of the evangelization as churches multiplied across Palestine and the Mediterranean world. What are we Christians to make of all this? Is there something here we can use?

Many educated Christians have been more secularized than they realize and are antagonistic to divine healing. They write it off as superstition and fraud; it leads people away from sound medicine and counts many as healed who are still sick. They say divine healing is a massive deception. They think that divine healing is using God for our own ends.

All Christians ought to think their way through this matter and realize that here is a power which a great many of us have not sufficiently used.

When healing in Christ's name has occurred and has attracted wide attention, multitudes can hear the gospel and many will obey it. This is the convincing witness of the New Testament and of modern history in many parts of the world, including the Western World.[2]

Early in my own life I had been taught that healing is not for today. So my Bible was a "not for today" version. Many promises for healing went unused in my life. A little teaching in my ministry would have given encouragement to people to experience Christ's provision for their health. I heard of healings and saw some healings, even as early as 1966 when the Lord healed Jane's eyes. But I was still blocked by unbelief and fear that I was stepping into a realm that lacked Biblical support and in which I lacked adequate experience.

As the Word of God opened to me with new freshness at Graceland and we saw repeated healings, I began to rethink this entire issue. This reappraisal convinced me that the healing ministry of Jesus is to be as much a part of His Body, the Church, as it was part of His life 2,000 years ago. He is unchanged. His power is not diminished, and where a climate of faith exists, He heals people.

A steady flow of healings began to characterize the services at Graceland, but healing was not magnified. Some at first had questions and were typically skeptical. Among the questioning group was Steve Marcum, Elvis and Virginia's son. Steve was a staff member effectively serving as recreational pastor. As the services extended, he had no problem adjusting a major summer recreational program. Yet to pray for the sick seemed like going too far in his practical mind.

In the many roles that he had played in athletics, Steve had injured his back. Though painful, it didn't prohibit him from fulfilling most of his duties. As he sat in the sound control both in the balcony one evening, he saw a friend go forward to be prayed for. Steve watched as deacons and others gathered to pray for his friend. He hurried out of the balcony to join them. He got there late and could not reach his friend so he laid his hand on the back of a deacon as a symbol of agreement for his friend's healing. As he stood there praying for his friend, the Lord healed his back. From that night on, Steve was one of the first ones to go to the altar to pray for people.

Healings occurred in a variety of forms: Some people were healed instantaneously, some were healed partially, some were healed through medical care, and some without medical assistance. Others came for healing and healing did not occur. The "mystery of godliness" is seen in the mystery of healing. A mystery contains both the known and unknown. In the unknown, the mysterious qualities of God are seen.

Why some are healed and others are not cannot be answered definitely. One of the reasons we do not see more healing lies in our systems of unbelief. In Mozambique, Roland and Heidi Baker see countless people healed. Their children in the orphanages are the primary praying agents for healing. Heidi makes the point that if they can teach the children faith before they are taught unbelief, they just believe the Lord for anything He has promised.[3]

One of the partial healings that occurred at Graceland was in the life of Dr. Fred Hubbs, pastor of Arlington Baptist Church in Jacksonville, Florida. I had known him in Missouri as a friend to pastors as he served as the Assistant Executive Secretary. His daughter Debbie attended the service and shared that her father was partially paralyzed and in great pain from a neurological disease.

Here is his own account, as published in *Fulness Magazine* in 1983:

> I was experiencing excruciating pain in my back and left leg to the degree that I was taking Percocet every four hours and wearing a T.E.N.S. Nerve Stimulator. The T.E.N.S. is a prescription item used to ease unbearable pain. It had been prescribed for me by a neurological doctor because of the severe pain.
>
> The night Jim Hylton called me in Jacksonville, Florida and invited me to come to the revival services I made excuses. I was extremely busy; I had been gone; and I guess

I felt if God wanted to heal me, He could heal me any place and anytime he chose. I was confident that He knew where I was since he had placed me at Arlington Baptist Church four years prior. But then Debbie called and then Elvis Marcum, the pastor, called. I felt God must be moving in a strong way for so many people to descend upon me. I mentioned it to our church and they were enthusiastic that I go and one of the deacons handed Shirley and me airline tickets.

On June 19, we went to Graceland. That Thursday evening will never be forgotten. I wanted to make the situation as difficult as possible, so I did not take a pain pill after 1:00 P.M. and I turned the T.E.N.S. machine off and suffered through the service that evening. After the service, Jim Hylton asked if we could have some fellowship in the pastor's study. Several of us gathered there.—I sat in a chair and the others gathered around me. Each prayed asking for forgiveness and cleansing, then they laid hands on me and prayed. I knew it would be embarrassing when I sat in the straight chair, for I would be unable to sit there more than five minutes. But I do not recall experiencing one pain during that time of prayer that must have lasted twenty to thirty minutes. I never experienced any more pain in that leg from that night until the present.

On that Thursday night we asked God to remove the pain from my leg and he did. We did not ask God to heal the disease that affects the joints and connecting tissues in my body. I still have the disease. I walk without pain, but I experience discomfort in other parts of my body because the disease does remain. —Our God is able, and I believe that what He had done for me is for His glory.

I had not planned to say anything to the church about my experiences. But, on Sunday morning before I hardly realized I was doing it, I gave my testimony to the church. It was received joyously. When the service ended and everyone had gone, I came through the auditorium and found Dr. Jerry Simpson, a professor at Luther Rice Seminary, waiting for me. Jerry had suffered from asthma for many years and had on this particular Sunday turned down a preaching engagement because he did not have enough breath to preach. He said, "Pastor, when you gave your testimony this morning, I was deeply moved in my soul, and I prayed and asked God to touch my body as He had yours. Immediately, I felt a cold shaft of air go all the way to the bottom of my lungs. I thought it was my imagination, so I sat and kept breathing deeply, and I breathed easily and completely without effort." Dr. Simpson has done well since then, and has even cut firewood in the winter. Another man, a Lebanese man, was touched that morning and now walks and moves with ease because God has touched his life.[4]

The rebounding effect of healing not only touches one life, but others who hear about the work that God has done. Looking back, I am amazed that we did not pray more comprehensively for Fred Hubbs. He did receive an extension of life, usefulness for the Lord, and had considerable freedom from pain.

A.B. SIMPSON ON HEALING

I do not want to belabor accounts of people being healed, but am going to share one more account to illustrate the variety of circumstances and ways God brings physical healing to his people.

A.B. Simpson was a man mightily used of the Lord in America and the world. As a Presbyterian, he formed a fellowship of pastors and churches who were on the same spiritual journey with a commitment to evangelism and missions. That fellowship eventually became one of the greatest "sending agencies" in the church, The Christian and Missionary Alliance. I think of that group of people as the "Oops Denomination." They never meant to be a denomination, so it was an "Oops!" Simpson wrote an excellent book on the subject of divine healing and was an advocate of the Church engaging in healing ministries. But he was not always so persuaded.

In the biography of A.B. Simpson, *Wingspread,* A.W. Tozer records this experience that was to shape Simpson's life and thinking:

> In the summer of 1881 A. B. Simpson visited Old Orchard, Maine, a famous summer re-sort and convention ground on the Atlantic Ocean. His heart and nerves had failed him and he moved about slowly in great weakness and bodily pain. Dr. Charles Cullis was con-ducting a gospel meeting in an amphitheater near the ocean side, and Mr. Simpson felt a desire to attend.... At the Cullis meetings he heard men and women testify to supernatural healing. His own great need compelled him to give close attention to those testimonies....

> However, he would not be taken in by the enthusiasm of those well-intentioned people. He must know for himself. "It drove me to my Bible," he testified. "I am so glad I did not go to man. At His feet alone, with my Bible open, and with no one to help or guide me, I became convinced that this was part of Christ's glorious Gospel for a sinful and suf-fering world, for all who would believe and receive His word."

So, one Friday afternoon, with a fallen log for an altar, he knelt and sought the face of God.

Suddenly the power of Christ came upon him. It seemed as if God Himself was beside him, around him, filling him and the sanctuary with the glory of His presence. "Every fiber in my soul," he said afterward, "was tingling with the sense of God's presence."

Stretching his hands toward the green vaulted ceiling he took upon himself the vow that saved him from an early grave, and—as subsequent developments revealed—changed the entire direction of his ministry and made him the greatest exponent of divine healing that the church has seen in a thousand years...

He would solemnly accept the truth of divine healing as a part of the word of God and the Gospel of Christ. He would take the Lord Jesus as his physical life, for all the needs of his body until all his life-work was done. He solemnly promised to use this blessing for the glory of God and the good of others.

He left that piney temple a man physically transformed. A few days later he went on a long hike into the country. This weakling minister for whom the grave had been eagerly waiting climbed a mountain three thousand feet high. The old trouble never visited him again.[5]

As this report from A.W. Tozer (one of the most respected spiritual leaders ever) indicated, the best way to find out how to respond to the truth of divine healing is to get in the presence of God and learn about healing from Him. While people still debate the issues and aspects of healing, Jesus is faithfully healing people throughout the world. A friend says, "It is a dangerous mentality that would prefer having all your theological questions answered instead of having all the needs of people met."

Wherever Jesus went, He took time to heal the sick. It is true He didn't heal all who were sick, just those who came to Him or those in whom He found faith. It is equally true He didn't save all of the lost, just those who believed in Him. The reasoning that is most common says, "Jesus didn't heal all the sick, so don't teach healing is available today." If carried to a consistent conclusion, we would teach, "Jesus didn't save everyone, so don't teach salvation is available today."

How extensive was His healing ministry?

> Then great multitudes came to Him, having with them the lame, blind, mute, maimed, and many others; and they laid them down at Jesus' feet, and He healed them. So the multitude marveled when they saw the mute speaking, the maimed made whole, the lame walking, and the blind seeing; and they glorified the God of Israel (Matthew 15:30-31).

Not only did Jesus heal wherever He went, but the early Church did the same:

And through the hands of the apostles many signs and wonders were done among the people. And they were all with one accord in Solomon's Porch. Yet none of the rest dared join them, but the people esteemed them highly. And believers were increasingly added to the Lord, multitudes of both men and women, so that they brought the sick out into the streets and laid them on beds and couches, that at least the shadow of Peter passing by might fall on some of them. Also a multitude gathered from the surrounding cities to Jerusalem, bringing sick people and those who were tormented by unclean spirits, and they were all healed (Acts 5:12-16).

Church life was so filled with the life of Christ that even the shadow of a man, Peter, contained the expressions of Christ's power. We do not cast such a shadow today. Our shadow sometimes contains shame and contradictions of His life within us. Unfortunately, we have become a mere shadow instead of the real substance of Christ's inhabited body on this earth.

HANDLING TREASURY NOTES FROM HEAVEN

No wonder the Christians of the world rush to any announcement of sightings of the substance of Christ's manifested presence. Lakeland, Florida, recently became the capital city of hope for the life of Jesus to be in evidence among His people. It is commendable that a believing pastor and a praying people were willing to share their heart hunger and faith with the Christian world. Christ's presence was manifested in Lakeland. His healing power did touch people and pastors, like my friend from Australia, and they were renewed in focus and faith. Even with the immaturity and inconsistencies of guest leaders of that expression, Christ was willing to share His life. He shares His life on the basis of grace and truth. Grace is sufficient to co-mingle His power with gross sin until truth prevails. Truth did prevail and issues were dealt with in the light of God's mercy accompanied by grace and truth.

Skeptics of healing experiences like Lakeland cry out against all healing emphasis. The real is never separated from the unreal. One of the basic approaches to detecting counterfeit money is to handle so many genuine, authentic bills that when the counterfeit is handled it is immediately detected. Sadly, we handle so few real treasury notes from Heaven that many times we can't detect the real from the counterfeit. Many have chosen to not handle any and thus avoid the mistakes of others. By refusing to handle Heaven's currency, we are like the church of Laodicea, *"You say, 'I am rich, with everything I want; I don't need a thing!' And you don't realize that spiritually you are wretched and miserable and poor and blind and naked"* (Rev. 3:17 TLB).

There are treasury notes from Heaven good for healing for ourselves as well as for others.

> *My advice to you is to buy pure gold from Me, gold purified by fire—only then will you truly be rich. And to purchase from Me*

> *white garments, clean and pure, so you won't*
> *be naked and ashamed; and to get medicine*
> *from Me to heal your eyes and give you back*
> *your sight* (Revelation 3:18 TLB).

Healing that Jesus so freely extended to others still comes from His life when He is permitted to express Himself through His Church. Our great need in the American church is to first accept His healing for us.

Many a church is in the intensive care unit. Closing of churches in once-prolific denominations is common. That is projected to increase.[6] Discouraged and disenfranchised pastors abound. Churches that are moved from critical care units are often left in a hospital wing and never enjoy full health again.

Jesus asked a man lame from birth *"Do you want to be well?"* (John 5:6). That is the question we must answer also. A sick church may refuse the power the Lord has sent to make it whole. A healthy church receives all the power available for it as well as for others.

When the Church is not really concerned about hurting people, it has no sense of the need for the supernatural. The institutional church is more concerned in maintaining credibility and fostering success and image. When we *"let this mind be in us that was in Christ"* (Phil. 2:5) and start ministering as He did, we will gladly welcome all the supernatural power available.

THE HEALTH CRISIS

America is facing a health crisis! Headlines and political pundits have highlighted that fact for years. Estimates go as high as 40 million Americans who are uninsured.[7] Most of the people of the world are not concerned about insurance. They are concerned about health. Insurance would not help them because medical services are not available. Every thinking and caring person whom I know voices their concern about this issue in our own nation. With the current economic crisis, even more people will potentially be in need of insurance.

Is health insurance what we need, or health assurance? Health insurance can be part of health assurance, but even insurance does not guarantee assurance. Too many times in my life time I have walked into intensive care units to visit patients whose main concern is not insurance, but healing. They want assurance from the Lord.

About two years ago I walked with some believing friends into the ICU of a major medical complex, Barnes Hospital, St. Louis, Missouri. The lady we went to pray with and anoint with oil was so weak I could barely hear her. Though very weak, her eyes glistened with excitement as she shared that angels had come to her in the night. Then she said, "They came again, and this time Jesus came with them." "What did He say?" I asked. "He said 'Jean, you may come home anytime,' but I told Him I wanted to live and see my grandkids."

Her believing husband, her loving friends, and I prayed for her to live within her rights as a child of God. The next morning her husband, who had slept on the couch in the lobby, went to her room and found her sitting up in the bed eating breakfast. Her blood oxygen level improved from almost requiring life support to normal. A few days later she was sent home, able to care for herself. In the space of a few hours she was enabled by the indwelling life of Christ to regain her strength and have freedom from the cancer that had filled her lungs. Her life was extended for over a year with that touch from the Lord. After a year, tests revealed that cancer had spread to her brain. With victory and readiness to meet the Lord, she experienced the ultimate healing by being lifted to His presence in Heaven.

Church life can be restored to a normal level. There are no issues in the contemporary Church that Jesus cannot transform. Both this woman and her husband believed that part of the reason for her healing for that year was for their church to be healed. Knowing that she would soon join the Lord, her last words to me on the phone were, "Please use my story to encourage others."

GOD PROVIDES HEALTH FOR HIS PEOPLE

Disease is not from God. Disease is an intrusion in a life that was designed by the Lord for healthy living. God does not inject people with disease germs. Every good and perfect gift comes from God (see James 1:17).

Under the Old Covenant, now upgraded and improved, God's people lived with none of the diseases of Egypt. That was His promise, *"You will have none of these diseases"* (Exod. 15:26). Two million people lived without the need of a doctor and in good health.

Healing is God's will. God wants us to prosper and be in good health as our souls prosper (see 3 John 2). A healthy soul contributes to a healthy body. Healing is an emergency measure God takes to restore our bodies to His original design. God wants us well. Divine health is His perfect plan. Divine health would not require healing.

Jesus taught us a foundational prayer, *"Pray your will be done on earth as it is in heaven"* (Matt. 6:10). There is no disease in Heaven. God's will on earth as a first choice is not an accommodation of disease. Disease is a permission that God grants until we operate in the level He initially intended.

If it is not God's will to heal, doctors would be at cross-purposes with God. God would be perpetuating disease, and doctors would be trying to prevent it. The reason we accommodate disease so readily is that, in the Western world, we pray for healing that doesn't occur and we are conditioned to unbelief.

Since all disease is a contradiction of the original design of God, why not allow the Lord to teach us as Jesus taught the disciples to declare the Kingdom is at hand by sharing His healing with others? Now is a great time to hear God out on the subject. Our own nation of America is now in need of health assurance.

If the Church will become normal as a healed, functioning Body of Christ, we can offer healing in a clinical approach. Healing involves both the supernatural and the natural. God built our bodies with healing agencies in various functions. One part of the body may be sharing its ability with other parts of the body that has a need.

One church I know well, Henderson Hills Baptist Church in Edmond, Oklahoma, offers medical services to people as part of its ministry. "The Ministry of Jesus" in that church is based on Luke 4:18-19. Jesus announced His own agenda. They believe He has not withdrawn His offer.

> *The Spirit of the Lord is upon me; He has*
> *appointed me to preach Good News to the poor;*

*He has sent me to heal the brokenhearted and
to announce that captives shall be released
and the blind shall see, that the downtrodden
shall be freed from their oppressors, and that
God is ready to give blessings to all who come
to Him* (Luke 4:18 TLB).

Henderson Hills is a church with as many doctors from the medical community in Oklahoma City as any church I know. With about 70 men and women who are committed to Christ and skilled in medical practice, they offer their services as a gift to people in need. It is a comprehensive ministry that includes counseling, a ministry to free people from bondages, dental services, and the medical specialties.

Other churches are combining the practical with supernatural. Instead of putting divine healing on the stage, the Church can awaken to Christ's way of healing the sick. He did not engage in "healing campaigns" or theatrical demonstrations. We can begin to teach every Christian to allow the life of Christ in them to create a Kingdom authority to heal people. If we can move from theatrics to clinical approaches, we can see America's current health crisis assisted, if not met.

Most cities in America have hospitals that bear the names of Presbyterian, Baptist, Catholic, Methodist, Episcopalian, and countless other church identities. The Church once offered a presence in the medical healing community. Few of those church-sponsored hospitals now operate under the guidance of the denomination whose name they bear. The big business of medical spreadsheets has altered the purpose for which they were started.

A summit could be called in America with health providers, doctors, clinicians, and men and women of faith to find solutions to the current needs in America. The Church could and should lead the charge.

Health assurance is available to all who will come to the presence of Jesus. His Kingdom is operative. Healing is part of His benefits to His Kingdom family. When sickness is healed by the person being lifted from their body into Christ's presence, no second-guessing or questioning of faith in action should occur. Going to Heaven is a complete and permanent healing. There is still a 100 percent mortality rate among us here. One of my heroes and dearest friends was a medical doctor who was healed of cancer and healed of surgical complications that put him in ICU longer than anyone in a hospital where he once served as Chief of Staff. Many years after the second dramatic healing, he developed Amyotrophic Lateral Sclerosis, or Lou Gehrig's, disease and later died. He was healed totally and permanently. His other healings were real, but did not preclude the diagnosis that came years later.

All the answers as to "why" await our seeing the Lord face to face. We do not need all the answers to act on what we do know. This friend was healed three times. Cancer was reversed in the first healing. Organs that failed following surgery were healed the second time. After many years when Lou Gehrig's disease developed, he found grace to face life while the usage of his body gradually diminished. Then healing came again. This time it was total and permanent.

Clinically, we can express the mind of Christ, extend the hand of Christ, and see the power of Christ evidenced in healing today. His Kingdom can come and healing will be part of that expression.

Chapter 6

WAGING WAR—A KINGDOM ENGAGEMENT

By the seventh week of the series of blessings at Graceland, it seemed logical to me to end the meetings. Each week required a careful review to see if the pastor and leaders were all agreed to extend yet again. Even more careful assessments seemed appropriate for week seven.

I was seeking to follow a theme for each week. "America is too Young to Die" seemed to be an appropriate theme for the birthday celebration of America on July 4, 1980. That theme was the title of a prophetic book by Leonard Ravenhill. Armed with that book, *The Light and the Glory* by Peter Marshal and David Manuel, and *The Dynamics of Spiritual Life* by Richard Lovelace, I was planning to pull salient quotes to document our spiritual heritage as a nation. The emphasis was to be that this nation born in spiritual awakening needed to be "born again" through spiritual awakening.

Charles G. Finney was well known for saying, "Fatigue is the enemy of revival." We soon learned to defeat that enemy by not scheduling services on Monday and Tuesday nights. Much personal ministry occurred during those "days off," but there was not the schedule of the morning and evening services that was the usual pattern. I would normally return to Fort Worth on Sunday afternoon and share at Lake Country Baptist Church on Sunday night. They graciously gave me away to this expression of God's demonstrated grace offering. On this weekend before the Fourth of July, I sensed a need to stay in Graceland and use all of Monday and Tuesday to be adequately prepared.

A TIME TO DEAL WITH SICKNESS AT HOME

Jane flew in from Fort Worth that afternoon to join me for what was assumed to be a final week. We would have two days of comparative rest and quiet as I studied, prayed, and became saturated with the word to be given that last week.

When I picked Jane up at the airport, she was a very sick lady. Three years before, she had been diagnosed as having low blood sugar, or hypoglycemia. Though she went with me to the service on Sunday night, she could hardly hold her head up. The fastest way to get her blood sugar up, apart from glucose, which required medical assistance, was honey. We started her on the honey immediately after the service closed. It was too late. She started vomiting, and we knew from past experience the progression to come.

So many healings had already occurred in the six weeks of services that I had become convinced that the Lord intended to heal her. Two other times the Lord had healed her, and those were times when she was aware of His leading and I was totally unaware (as I described in the story of the healing of her eyes). When I shared with her that I believed the Lord wanted to heal her, her response was negative since the Lord hadn't spoken to her. Then she realized the Lord was teaching me to claim healing for her. Both of us were excited and were eager to see the healing take place.

Despite our hope for healing, this new attack was very discouraging. We prayed and committed it to the Lord and got the best rest possible with her weakened condition and nausea. The next morning the condition was worse. From past experiences we knew that, at this stage, the only way to stabilize her was to get some glucose. Virginia Marcum called their family doctor, and he instructed us to get to the emergency ward of the local hospital.

A strong summer thunderstorm was developing when Virginia arrived at the motel. We drove through rain-drenched streets where water was so deep it occasionally ran over the curbs. Progress was very slow. Intermittently, Jane would need to vomit, and I would open the door and hold her head as she vomited outside.

What I had so anticipated as a relaxed day for study and finely honing the messages for the week became a "comedy of errors." Caught in the deluge of rain, watching Jane suffer in weakness, nausea, and some pain, I was no longer a man of faith or patience. All anticipation of healing was gone from me. Rain drenched her hair as she leaned out the door to get rid of anything left in her stomach. My faith was drenched more than her hair.

When we arrived at the hospital, I was sure that my vast medical knowledge from the *Reader's Digest* would assist the nurses in speeding up the process to salvage part of this important day for my preparation. The nurse was not impressed with my knowledge and did not take the obvious steps to give her the glucose.

Instead, we went through all the formalities and forms of the past medical history. Blood samples were taken and blood analysis begun. They restudied her medical history. After most of the day had elapsed, the nurse came in and said, "Mr. Hylton, we can't explain this, but her blood sugar is normal. Due to the extreme nausea we are going to give her the glucose, hoping it will aid in stopping the vomiting." The simple steps I had suggested hours earlier were taken. Jane responded immediately and the nausea ceased. I called Virginia and she graciously returned us to the motel in the late afternoon. Soon the doctor called to report, "Mr. Hylton, this is a puzzling case. Mrs. Hylton's blood sugar is 118 in the normal range. We have given her glucose, but not because the tests indicated she needed it." I thanked him for his time and attention to her case and shared with Jane what he said.

I was planning to get back to the book I was reading and the preparation I was making when Jane responded with elation. "Don't you see what this means?" she asked. "I'm healed! The Lord has healed me! My blood sugar count has never been higher than 60 or 70 at the most for several years."

My visions of her vomiting out the door of the car were still graphically embedded in my mind. I muttered in unbelief and cynicism, "Yes, you have had all the appearances of being healed all day."

"But I had asked the Lord to give me verification that my blood sugar was normal," she explained. "This is the way He chose to do it."

Indeed, it had been the Lord's way to verify the healing. In spite of my having once believed and then having spent most of that day out of step with the Lord, she was healed and has remained healed of low blood sugar for 29 years. It was a twofold lesson. It was not my faith that carried the day, but the Lord's faithfulness. It was not my attitude that was exemplary, but His own heart of love reaching out to a precious lady and the greatest Christian I have ever known.

That series of events should have alerted me to the probability that this was not going to be an ordinary week. An attack had come. A testing had occurred. I got a low grade, but Jesus remained faithful.

In fact, I was in that third of the class that makes the upper two-thirds possible. It was not about me or dependent on me. It was all about Him and His faithfulness. Victory was shared and Jane was healed, but what lay ahead would "blow my mind."

A BATTLE STARTED IN ANOTHER STORM

War was about to break out in unmistakable confrontations. The Lord sent a retired general to be there when the assault came. Elvis Marcum and I had prayed about bringing in a speaker to speak on America's perceived condition and agreed on General Albion Knight, retired from the United

States Army. He was a godly man who was also an ordained Episcopal minister.

General Knight arrived on Wednesday night, July 3, in the heat and humidity that the Ohio River Valley is famous for. Inside the beautiful auditorium, a pleasant coolness greeted a crowd that packed out the house. At Elvis Marcum's request, I introduced General Knight. No sooner had he begun to speak then a thunderstorm struck. Wind and lightening were unleashed in the area. A lightning bolt knocked out the electricity with a boom like a bomb blast. We were plunged into pitch darkness as the temperature inside began to sweep upward, creating a sauna-like atmosphere. A heavy, sticky warmth settled like a net.

I was seated on the platform and could see the trees outside against the lightning flashes in the sky. They were bending nearly to the ground and tossing violently in the wind. I thought the trees would uproot at anytime. Sheets of rain driven by the wind slammed against the front doors and began running into the foyer. Without the aid of the sound system, Albion Knight adjusted readily and pitched his voice to be heard by the 1,500 in attendance.

My awareness of the storm outside was suddenly eclipsed by a growing awareness of a storm inside, the storm of satan's assault. I had heard men hypothesize that satan can garner a storm to interrupt what God is doing. But that night I was totally convinced that this was an assault from the enemy.

I recalled that Jesus had rebuked a storm, which indicated that he knew it was from satan (see Mark 4:39). I reasoned that a storm from His Father in Heaven would have never been rebuked, but welcomed. I began asking for guidance from the Lord. General Knight was speaking, and since he was an Episcopalian, I wondered if he would agree with rebuking storms.

An auxiliary power source was brought from an adjoining building, and a small bulb in a trouble light was used to dimly illuminate the speaker. Even the small light enabled people to see General Knight, who continued to speak. That transition gave me a chance to do what was stirring in me.

I asked General Knight to let me speak for a moment, and he graciously encouraged me to do so. As I stood there that night, I addressed the enemy in the name of the Lord Jesus Christ. I claimed the blood of Christ over us and addressed the storm in the name of Jesus Christ, demanding that the enemy withdraw the attack. My own personal assessment was that if I did not stand that night in the authority of Christ, I would face defeat from the enemy the rest of my life. I stood because I sensed I was standing in Christ and His authority. The storm subsided and the Lord's presence again filled the auditorium.

As had been true for nights, it was a service attended by the Lord's presence even though there were the many distractions of the violent storm. Albion Knight gave an excellent word on America's need to return with a humble heart to the Lord. In the limited light and the very warm auditorium, we closed the service without a long ministry time.

ENCOUNTERING A DEMONIC MANIFESTATION

The next night we gathered again; it was July 4. I shared from the spiritual history of America using the book *The Light and the Glory*. That account documents that demonic strongholds threatened the existence of the colonies. But Cotton Mather went to the pulpit to boldly expose the enemy and to take a stand that turned defeat into victory. Here is the account of Peter Marshal and David Manuel:

> The Bible makes it clear that there are only two sources of supernatural power: God and Satan. And in the spiritual realm as in geopolitics, there is not such a power vacuum; where Light reigns, darkness is banished. But when the Light dims, the shades of night gather in the wings, waiting. The candle flame grows weaker still and begins to flicker; the darkness holds its breath.

> As the seventeenth century drew to a close, so enfeebled had the affluent Christianity of the Puritans again become, that the supernatural manifestations of Satan's power—occultism, witchcraft, poltergeist phenomena (demons and mischief) et al.— were coming out into the open. Witches began hanging out their shingles, as it were, letting it quietly be known that they could cure warts, and straighten toes and mix love potions (all white magic, for the come-ons; the black magic—the hexing, the cursing, the spell binding would come later). And the gullible, the unwary, the hopeless turned to this source of power; and more and more

people began to come to the "knowing ones" for advice and counsel.

Of the contemporary accounts of this sudden holocaust of satanic activity, Cotton Mather's was the most comprehensive. This was not because he obsessed with the occult (as modern anti-Puritans would have us believe.), but simply because he was one of the few ministers strong enough in the faith to come against Satan and reign supremely confident of victory. And because of this, everyone came to him with his supernatural problems—as if he were the only fireman in a town of straw houses.

As we read these ancient accounts of some of the things that happened, we were frankly stunned; cases of demonic possession and poltergeist phenomena were nothing new to us, but never had we heard of whole towns literally infested with invisible beings, or anything to compare with the intensity of their malevolence. And God had allowed it, as a warning, and to shake the Christian settlers out of their acute spiritual apathy.[2]

I gave that account verbatim that night and brought a strong message on spiritual warfare and victory in Christ. As the invitation was given, people came to the front with the usual eagerness. Some came to know the Lord. Some came to yield their lives more fully to the Lord. Some were coming for healing (by this time I was giving invitations for people to come for prayer to be healed).

I had grown comfortable watching people be healed. Though we placed no major emphasis on healing, many were being healed. Some came for healing and went away just as they came, but never with an indication that they were second class or at fault because of little or no faith. The deacons and church leaders had grown confident praying for the sick at the altar. Elvis Marcum was at ease doing so from the beginning since he had experienced healing in his own body. Most of the time I did not join in praying for the people, but could better direct the continuation of the decision and ministry time.

That night a young Puerto Rican rolled himself forward in his wheelchair from the deaf section where people signed to the deaf each service. He was a handsome, bearded young man with a long, afro hairstyle.

When he arrived at the front, he signed to the interrupter that he wanted me personally to pray for him. I was at ease praying for the sick, but I had never prayed for a man in a wheelchair who was deaf and mute. As I looked at the man, I asked the Lord to guide and give me faith.

Acting in faith sometimes builds faith, and by the time I reached the wheelchair, I was really expecting the Lord to do something special for the man named Ozzie. I reached out and laid my hands lightly on his shoulders while he sat bent forward with his head bowed in prayer. No sooner had my hands touched his shoulders than his body began to quiver and then convulse under my hands. The violent wrenching of his body all but threw him out of the chair. Had I not grabbed his shoulders with all the strength of my hands and arms, he would have been thrown to the floor.

I knew immediately that a demon spirit had manifested in him and was creating this convulsing reaction. I was also aware that by this time the commotion had the attention of most people in the auditorium. My startled reaction was a reflex action as I commanded the demons to release him. What I lacked in faith I made up for in volume. Demons are not hard of hearing, but in my spontaneous reaction I yelled out of my own inexperience and intimidation. To my considerable relief, Ozzie settled back into the wheelchair as the convulsions stopped.

Scanning the crowd quickly, I saw a stunned look of dismay and fear on most faces. Had there been time to think about it in advance, I, too, would probably have been scared. Two pastors from Louisville who had come to monitor the service were heading hastily up the aisle. They never returned.

ANOTHER SOLDIER TO LEAN ON

As I stood beside Ozzie's wheelchair, checking on how he was doing, I looked up and saw a man standing directly across from me. He was standing tall with his chin jutting out as if in defiance against the demonic forces that attacked Ozzie. No fear was on his face, just confidence. A great sense of strength came to me in that one glance for I sensed that if the manifestations began again, I would not battle alone. There was another soldier to lean on.

Calm had returned to Ozzie so I returned to the platform and continued the invitation that lasted another 30 minutes or so. My eyes would return often to the face of the man still standing at Ozzie's chair. Later, he sat down on the front row. Before the invitation ended, I went down and knelt beside him and said, "Those demons didn't leave, they just hid." "I know," he replied with confidence. "How do you know about demons?" I asked. "Oh, I have had experience with these things," was his simple reply.

"Who are you?" was my next blunt question.

"I am Milton Green, a carpet cleaner from Cleveland, Tennessee," was his unassuming answer. Then he continued, "I came here to be part of the witnessing team." General Knight was there one night. This general in the Lord's army, named Milton Green, arrived the next night, planning to stay three days. He stayed several weeks.

On the same night I gave the historic account of Cotton Mather's influence on early America, a man with equal authority in facing the demonic had shown up at Graceland. He was not a man of formal training, but he was a man who pressed against God's heart and soaked his mind in the Word of God. He looked at me with eyes filled with love and faith and said, "Oh, it's in my heart to help that poor tormented man in that wheelchair." It was arranged for Milton and me to meet with Ozzie and the interpreter.

I asked Milton to take the lead. He started at the right place and asked Ozzie about his relationship to Christ. Ozzie said in sign language that he had never received Christ as his Lord and Savior. He did so and became our brother. An immediate change came in his countenance. The hard, desperate look of hurt and bitterness left his face.

The Marshal and Manuel account of demonic activity in early America found in *The Light and the Glory* was soon to be in evidence in the Graceland experience. Through further conversations, we learned that Ozzie had grown up in a witch's home in New York. All his life he had been subjected to séances and every conceivable practice of witchcraft. He described how he became involved in a cult. In an unusual accident, he fell and broke his back while fighting with a friend over a pack of cigarettes. His back was injured permanently, and he was left in a wheelchair, deaf and mute. Obviously, this was no ordinary case.

On the following Tuesday evening, no service was scheduled so Milton and I joined the Graceland staff of pastors to minister to Ozzie. Doris, who was always available to sign the words to Ozzie, was also present to enable communication. Milton sat down across from Ozzie. He reminded him of the victory Christ had won for him and that he was now a new creation in Christ, quoting verse after verse of Scripture. Prayer followed as members of that selected team began praying.

With authority that came with knowing Scripture and from his own experience of being set free from torment, Milton commanded the demon spirits to come to attention. Immediately, the countenance of Ozzie changed to a grotesque hideous face mirroring hatred and defiance. The demon powers then threw Ozzie from the wheelchair in a levitated manner halfway across the large room. He was thrown at least 15 feet past Milton and me. When Ozzie hit the floor, Milton was right behind him to help him up into a sitting position on the floor. Milton sat down cross-legged directly in front of Ozzie and commanded the powers of darkness to obey the authority of Jesus Christ.

No horror movie ever captured a face so grotesque as the manifested demons. With supernatural power, the demons began blowing gales of wind from Ozzie's lungs. Gale-force wind, with even the same accompanying sound, began blowing directly into Milton's face. Milt's hair was blowing straight back as if he was giving a weather report in the midst of hurricane winds. Milt would calmly say, "I have no fear of you, demon. I am the righteousness of God in Christ. You cannot hurt me."

Resorting to another intimidating tactic the demonic powers began snapping Ozzie's head straight back and hurling it right at Milton's face. Ozzie's afro hair was flying wildly. From his lungs the same enormous volume of air was being released and occasionally a hissing sound was heard in the rush of wind. Milt had but one response. He sat perfectly calm with his eyes locked into Ozzie's.

As Ozzie's head was snapped back and hurled at Milton's, his face would come within a half inch of Milton's. As if hitting an invisible shield, Ozzie's head would snap to a stop. I stood beside Milton and studied the most remarkable thing I had ever seen the Lord do with a man. Milt never blinked even an eyelash as that head covered with the massive outcropping of hair was hurled at his face. His courage was unrelenting and uncompromising. This encounter with powers of darkness made a John Wayne movie look like child's play. An anointing of the Lord was so strong on Milton that he was unconscious of much of what he was doing.

What I have documented for the first time was a turning point for me in warfare. When confronting demonic manifestations, I was always uncomfortable and intimidated. The demons were always only a little bit more afraid than I was (though I should not have feared at all). That night, I realized that the power of Christ is in us and is fully shared with us. This detailed account is given to inform the reader of the authority every follower of Christ possesses.

Soon the powers of darkness began releasing their hold on Ozzie's body. His face relaxed and another presence began to be evident in his countenance, the presence of Christ's life within him. Freedom came to Ozzie and we helped him back into his wheelchair.

The time that followed was one of the greatest worship experiences I have ever known before or since. The glory of God filled that room, and we sensed the power and presence of Jesus doing what He had announced He had come to do—set captives free.

The experience that evening was allowed so we could visualize the diabolical nature of the enemy. In no way should this account lead anyone to believe this was normal or to be expected in dealing with the powers of darkness. I believe the Lord allows such manifestations to teach beginners and unbelievers. Instead of deliverance being a ghoulish or dreaded engagement, it is really a very beautiful and normally quiet engagement of declaring victory for the person in need. The bondage-breaking teaching of Dr. Neil Anderson is excellent in granting people their emancipation. His methods primarily utilize the cancellations of any agreements made with the enemy, the reclaiming of any ground given to him, and the renewed submission of all areas of life to Christ.[3]

In the days that followed, Ozzie became increasingly joyful. Though I had expected his hearing and speech to be restored, they were not. Many people at Graceland prayed and believed that Ozzie would be totally healed, and feeling did return partially to his legs and back. Ozzie was part of enabling people to realize that Jesus intends to drive out the works of darkness. He was no longer tormented in his mind or body. A joyful man experienced a meaningful relationship with Christ.

FROM FREEDOM TO BONDAGE
OF ANOTHER KIND

Countless people's lives were greatly enriched by the ministry of Milton Green in Graceland. High-profile ministers' lives and ministries were salvaged through his desire to see captives set free. Unfortunately, the Church was so devoid of understanding in spiritual warfare that Milt was suddenly thrust on the stage and made an expert on everything. His understanding of warfare, which was so much greater than most people's, was still incomplete. Though his heart was pure, his understanding of many issues was limited.

The war he waged with powers of darkness, he extended to flesh and blood, which is clearly not a source of attack. Since we do not *"wrestle with flesh and blood"* (Eph 6:12), entering that wrestling match is at best a waste of time and at worst an assault on those needing our love and understanding. Though he reached conclusions not supported in the Scripture he loved, later he came to see the need for extending love and grace. Having often found companionship with the law more than with grace, he eventually returned to the cross and to the completed work of Christ.

Not too long before his death, he returned to Lake Country Baptist Church with a new joy in the freedom he had found and asked for forgiveness for his attitudes and judgments. That forgiveness was granted by all of us who loved him and appreciated his zeal for people to know freedom in Christ. His last days on this earth were filled with love, joy, and peace in the presence of Christ.

SPIRITUAL WARFARE IS A
REAL BATTLE FRONT

Jesus did not duck the issues of demonic activities. His authority over their powers was so complete that he likened their displacement to God's finger flipping them aside. *"But if I cast out demons with the finger of God, surely the kingdom of God has come upon you"* (Luke 11:20).

Peter Marshal and David Manuel clearly stated the case. "The Bible makes it clear that there are only two sources of supernatural power: God and Satan."[4] If we are going to welcome the supernatural power of God, we can expect the supernatural power of satan to be in evidence. They cannot exist together. God's power always has the ascendancy. Displacement of the enemy from his trespassing position is part of Kingdom expansion. For God's Kingdom to expand, an opposing Kingdom must be displaced.

Lest I leave the impression that demonic activity, which is usually oppression or obsession, not possession, occurs only in a person with a background like Ozzie, I will take space to describe one more instance. A lady who served on the secretarial and scheduling staff of Graceland had a great background. With a gifted mind that was close to photographic, she had memorized most, if not all, of the New Testament.

Francis Schaffer was her hero, and she had read everything he wrote and memorized most of it.

While a student at Vanderbilt University, she naively attended a séance out of curiosity. She saw the supernatural in what she considered harmless examples of various phenomena. Later, she began hearing voices in her mind. She repressed all of this and moved forward in her life. Her marriage to a man in the military was a good marriage. They had two boys.

As the services progressed at Graceland, she became more and more ill at ease, though she was pleased the Lord was touching and changing people. While sitting in the services, she would have compulsions at times to stand and shout during the messages, "It is a lie, don't believe this!"

The urge was so strong one night she clasped her hands over her mouth and ran from the auditorium. Later, she was awakened in the night with an obsession to get a knife from the kitchen and kill her sleeping sons. Frightened by this and knowing she had a deep-seated problem, she came to me and shared her bizarre thoughts.

While another staff member and I talked and prayed with her, she quickly gained her freedom. She took back the ground she had given during the séance at Vanderbilt University and affirmed her faith and commitment to Christ. Those powers of darkness assaulting her were quickly dispelled. The account I have just given is more typical of the power of Jesus to dispel the demonic assignment as if the finger of God flipped them away.

Don't assume that demonic activity cannot be very intellectual or very outwardly acceptable, as in the case of being on a church staff. What should also be clear is that victory has been won for each person. It is the power of Christ's presence that provokes and discloses the enemy. We don't need to go looking for the enemy. Our role is not to search and destroy. We are not looking for a fight, but we are not running from one, either. Our armor does not include a back plate for retreat, but a breastplate to face the enemy fully equipped. We are not told to become strong. Our instructions are to be strong in the Lord (see Eph. 6:10). He is our strength and we are strong.

"The power of God for salvation" (Rom. 1:16) contained in the Gospel of Christ causes demons to take a hike. We don't have to do spiritual mapping for every fortress to be found and destroyed. Neither biblical truth nor experiences that I have had require us to take a spiritual survey to locate all the enemy's strongholds in order to gain the victory. Heaven's surveillance system will reveal and flush the enemy out of hiding.

Prayer has been likened to the Air Force bombing out the fortresses of the enemy. Ground troops are necessary to occupy the land. Without prayer and discernment, needless casualties occur. These assaults on God's army are persistent. Knowing that we are fighting a battle already won by Christ on the cross, we are to fight in confidence and in strength.

WHAT THE LORD CAN DO

In the days of the Lord visiting West Plains, Missouri, in the 1960s, a lady came for an appointment in my study. As she shared her story of personal pain and guilt, I was suddenly visited by the Lord's presence in a way I had never known. I was sitting behind my desk, and she was across the room in the carefully appointed new office. I could see her, but could not hear her. Knowing I was keeping an unprecedented schedule of three to four hours of sleep a night, yet not being tired, I first thought I might be having a heart attack. Then I saw her scream, but still couldn't hear her, and she quickly ran out the side door.

As that strong presence, like enormous G's from a private jet aircraft in a takeoff, held my body in the chair, I could not move. After probably 15 to 20 minutes, I could move and hear again. I went looking for the lady. I found her in the church auditorium. With a radiant face, she shared two things.

She said, "I saw the Lord's presence on you and was frightened." I ran to the auditorium and knelt over there pointing to the front row of seats. Then she said almost casually, "Demons left me and I am free!"

At that time, I was a very rationalistic person who did not believe that demons existed. A professor of Bible had explained they were psychological problems identified as demonic spirits, and I had bought that lie. So, while my mind debated what she had said, my heart rejoiced that she was free.

Indeed she was freed, but not because of my understanding or participation. I served best by being plastered to my chair by Christ's presence while He did the work. The same demonstration of God's power can free individuals, churches, regions, cities, and nations from every assignment of the enemy. We do not need to understand everything in order to be more than conquerors.

Dr. John Wesley White, then an associate of the Billy Graham Association and now in Heaven, told me privately that he thought one of the most important books written for this generation was *The Adversary* by Mark I. Bubeck.

While serving as a pastor, Mark Bubeck discovered his daughter was being assaulted by demons. He describes the victory that followed through using sound biblical methods. In the foreword, John Wesley White writes,

> What we used to think was the special monopoly of primitive peoples—like the pagan barbarians of the Congo or the heathen-hearted savages of Borneo Jungles—has moved into fashionable suburbia. Voodoo, fortune telling, black magic, witchcraft, poltergeistism, spiritism with mediums, parapsychology clinics (which often are no more nor less than séances with professors as the mediums)—they're everywhere. It's not legal to have Christianity in sharp focus in academia, but the devil—the red carpet has been rolled out to him! Demonizing denizens seem to be the highest style today.[5]

Too long the Church has played in the consolation bracket where losers play. Weapons of warfare that are "smart weapons" belong to us. We can wage war, claiming a victory and declaring a victory that is already won. Our intelligence reports have been flawed. Our weaponry is often the outdated weaponry of traditions. A new anointing brings new courage and faith.

With the finger of God, Jesus assaulted demons. This same authority is resident in us because of His residing presence. His Kingdom is "presenced" because He is present. When Jesus goes into action, His Kingdom is in evidence. Powers of darkness are helpless before the authority of Christ. A part of the encompassing rule of Christ is exercised when He continues to destroy the works of the devil.

Chapter 7

LOSING THE WAR IN THE WRONG BATTLE

Friendly fire has created many of the current casualties among American Christians. The devil does not need to do much to defeat us. We can destroy ourselves with very little help from anyone else. Supernatural power from an enemy isn't needed. Propaganda from faulty information becomes our current intelligence report. We are engaged in battle, but often we fight the wrong enemy.

A part of my compulsion to write this perspective was born out of very recent experiences. These experiences occurred in two troubled churches. One was head-over-heels in debt with a small group of faithful people trying to hang on. They became stable with financial strength born out of allowing the Lord to offer His leadership and accompanying blessing.

The other church, already divided, was further fractured when a leader left, using divisive words and accusations. Divisions and power-plays for control were already there. But the leader's lack of graciousness while leaving precipitated a crisis. With a broken heart, I walked with godly, open-hearted people who were engaged in organizational battles and accompanying battle fatigue. Attorneys were asked to accompany members as consultants to advise them as to what they could or couldn't say in a business meeting. In that atmosphere, the moderator of the church didn't allow much to be said and stifled needed information from being given. Fortunately, those battle lines were dissolved before I got there, but the hurt and distrust remained.

Splintering occurred as a group left the church in protest. Offended and wounded people remained. Like in any train wreck, casualties occurred. Body parts and body bags were strewn all over the site. People of great quality and devotion to the Lord remained in the church and began a healing process. In that setting, I saw a part of church life I had never seen before.

Revival was seen as a possible solution for that troubled church. Indeed, revival as we have known it would alter some of the issues of the contemporary Church. So, one of the questions I was forced to ponder was, "What will a revived church look like?"

That church, made up mostly of the greatest people I have ever come to know, is not the reason for my conclusions. They are but typical of the condition of Church life generally. So little genuine Church life exists in the contemporary American church that to revive such a Church would only increase a system's failure. It is the system that is flawed, and reviving the system will only increase a faulty system.

It is my studied conclusion, meaning I have given it exhaustive consideration, that only a small percentage of what we are doing in the average church is really Church life. The percentages fall along these lines. About 25 percent of Church life is an expression of Christ's Body on this earth. (Several informed leaders think I am generous with this percentage.) Some of His life is on display and being shared with others. Another 25 percent is an organization that follows a business or corporate model, with finances and attendance as the primary standards of success. Yet another 25 percent is a political party membership in which sides are created on almost every issue, with accompanying power-plays. Still another 25 percent is a religious order dedicated to perpetuating the traditions created from the past.

These are the battle lines drawn in today's American Church, as I observe it. Even churches that gave up on traditional structure and became independent often take on the same characteristics under different names. Denominational churches are not at fault. Nondenominational churches soon take on their own traditions. Good, godly people are not at fault.

Our systems obscure our view of Jesus. Having lost sight of Him, we can't see His Kingdom. We are engaged in church building instead of Kingdom building, and the results are little real Church and a lot of real conflict.

A seminary president in a major denomination said a few years ago, "I am declaring a holy war!" The only thing unusual about his announcement was the fact it *declared* a war. Most holy wars are never declared, but fought to the death.

Why are there holy wars? Are these the same battle lines Jesus confronted? Holy wars are religious wars! Religion creates inward conflict and results in outward conflict. Christian religion without a Spirit-led relationship with Christ is no different than any other religion. It is a structure of beliefs and practices that are done in devotion to the God of the religion. The god of Christian religion is tradition. Though the tradition may be rich and heart-warming, if it is an outward form without a personal relationship to the living Lord, it is just a religion under a new name. Holy war, or jihad, is not limited to the Middle East. Sorrowfully, more holy wars may rage in America than anywhere.

My experience on several battle fronts and across several decades of wars and rumors of wars leads me to this conclusion. We make an enemy out of those who are our brothers and sisters, or those who could be. Instead of fighting the one who came to steal, kill, and destroy (see John 10:10), we fight each other. Jesus came to destroy the works of the devil (see 1 John 3:8). He has never changed His mission. That same assignment is ours.

Our battle is waged over issues that are not the real issues. These issues Jesus called "wineskins" or traditions. When challenged by the Pharisees about His choice of Matthew, a tax collector, as a disciple and His practice of eating with "sinners," He answered in story form. He described how old garments do not get new patches and old wine skins won't hold new wine (see Matt. 9:16-17). These traditions grow out of what may have started as a fresh work of God. Once they lose their initial purpose, they become "wineskins of tradition."

Every awakening precipitates a "wineskin war" because old wineskins begin to crack and tear from the energy of fermenting new wine. Threatened wineskins must be defended by those whose commitment is to a "cause" rather than to the Kingdom.

Many issues become the announced focus that people divide and war over. Some cry "doctrinal error," some cry "denominational disloyalty," and some cry "excesses instead of balance." But behind the protest, there is usually a threatened existence of a wineskin that no longer flexes under Christ's rule.

Wineskins have many expressions. It may be geographical territory, the cause of a ministry, a denominational standard, or a tradition that has become an idol to be followed rather than the truth God has spoken.

A TALE OF THREE KINGS IS A TALE TO ALL KINGS

Author and gifted thinker Gene Edwards wrote a classic book, *A Tale of Three Kings,* describing the battle that rages among people over territorial rights.[1] Organizational power and titles adorn and enhance people in the eyes of others. Edwards's tale of three kings is a "tale" that is not fictional, but an account of three biblical characters.

Saul reigned with the crown of a king, but without the heart of a king. David lived first without a king's crown, but with the heart of a king. Absalom had neither the heart nor the crown of a king, but was willing to kill his father David for the crown. Saul died with a crown, but never had the king's heart. David died with both the heart and crown of a true king. Absalom died with neither in his attempt to gain the crown.

Every leader's story is told in one of the three kings. Some gain power as did Saul, but never experience the purity of a Kingdom heart. Some gain purity in heart as did David and then experience the power of the Kingdom of God in operation. Some like Absalom allow ambition and selfish desires for power to obsess them. They lose their lives in the quest of what cannot be achieved, but can only be received as an offering of grace from God.

David's reign was the picture of the future reign of Christ. David's reign was also the picture of the Church operating in the worship and works of the Holy Spirit. When Kingdom power was reported among the Gentiles to the Jerusalem church, a council was called. James spoke to the council and cited the work of God among the Gentiles as being the evidence of David's tabernacle being restored:

> And to this agree the words of the prophets; as it is written, "After this I will return, and will build again the tabernacle of David, which is fallen down; and I will build again the ruins thereof, and I will set it up: that the residue of men might seek after the Lord, and all the Gentiles, upon whom My name is called,' says the Lord, who does all these things" (Acts 15:15-17 NKJV).

During David's reign, provision was made for the Lord to reign. The Tabernacle of David was created to house the Ark of the Covenant, where the Lord was present. It was the presence of the Lord, not the prominence of David, that was the primary characteristic of that Kingdom.

Every anointed person and every anointed ministry has the capability of building a kingdom. That kingdom will either be the Kingdom of God or the kingdom of the cause created by that person or ministry.

Many denominations begin with anointed people and anointed ministry. Either in those anointed ones or in those who followed them, a trend arose that led them to champion their own cause rather than the cause of the coming Kingdom and the will of God being done on earth as it is in Heaven. Those with worn, brittle wineskins have been part of over 200 denominations since the reformation. A reformation of the reformation would be timely.

GOOD PEOPLE CAN GO BAD

Saul was a formidable man. He was a distinguished leader who stood head and shoulders above other men. Anointing is a special enablement from God. Saul received that enabling along with his natural qualities (see 1 Sam. 10:1).

Two kingdoms appear to everyone who is anointed in ministry. Those two kingdoms were clear to Jesus. As soon as He was anointed with the Holy Spirit, the devil offered Him the kingdom of this world. He chose the Kingdom of God that was already within Him. All who come to the Kingdom as part of their destiny must make a choice as Jesus did. He chose God's Kingdom coming and God's will being done.

Saul is the tragic example of a king who made the opposite choice. Anointed with eyes to see the Kingdom and empowered to enforce the Kingdom, he lacked a heart for the Lord to reign through him. That lack of commitment to let the Lord reign is described in one revealing verse: *"Let us bring the ark of our God back to us; for we have not inquired at it since the days of Saul"* (1 Chron. 13:3). During the 40 years of Saul's reign, the ark of God, where God's presence resided, was never sought or appreciated.

Only once in 40 years did Saul desire to be before the Lord's presence in the ark. His desire then came out of a crisis. While his son Jonathan and Jonathan's armor bearer fought the Philistines, Saul asked to see the ark. Desperation drove him to consider the possibility of the Lord's presence being a means of protection (see 1 Sam. 14:18).

The ark was brought to Saul as he heard the sounds of battle. He quickly dismissed the ark to give attention to the Philistines. *"...So Saul said to the priest, 'Never mind; let's get going'"* (1 Sam. 14:19 NLT).

Several things are clear about the thoughts of Saul:

1. He feared the Philistines more than he valued the presence of God. The noise he heard was the noise of the Philistines killing each other.

2. Saul was unwilling to wait before the Lord's presence. A bad habit of not "waiting on the Lord" was not broken in a crisis. Forty years of neglecting the Lord was not corrected in a few minutes.

3. Saul was unwilling to let God speak to him. When he could not hear God, he depended

on his own counsel and the counsel of
other men. This is the error of all people
who value their kingdom over God's.

The final neglect of God's Kingdom on Saul's part led to
his forfeiture of the anointing to reign. The once good man
became a mad man. Faith and humility were gone from Saul.
Fear possessed him. The spears he neglected to use against the
Philistines and feared to use against Goliath, he chose to use
against David (see 1 Sam. 18:10-11).

HOW GOD MAKES ONE "FIT FOR A KING"

Two kings and two kingdoms were present in Saul's palace
at the same time. Saul's troubled mental state could only be
quieted when David was present playing the harp. The melody
of his heart reproduced on a harp brought calm to the discord
of Saul's confused heart.

Saul was a king that people wanted. He had a crown on his
head. David was a king that God wanted. He had a crown in
his heart for God's Kingdom. Saul's heart was full of madness.
David's heart was full of the melody of God's love for His king.

The inimitable style and insight of Gene Edwards illu-
mines how real king's hearts are created:

Unlike everyone else in spear throwing history, David did not know what to do when a
spear was thrown at him. He did not throw
Saul's spears back at him. Nor did he make
any spears of his own and throw them.

> Something was different about David. All he did was dodge.
>
> David never got hit. Gradually, he learned a very well-kept secret. He discovered three things that prevented him from ever being hit. One, never learn anything about the fashionable, easily-mastered art of spear throwers. Two, stay out of the company of all spear throwers. And three, keep your mouth tightly closed. "In this way, spears never touch you, even when they pierce your heart."[2]

The art of dodging spears was David's unique preparation to be a good king. He, too, came to the Kingdom for such a time as this (see Esther 4:14), but he always knew whose Kingdom it was and how it operated. He knew it was a Kingdom where forgiveness is granted and records of ill deeds are erased.

Spear dodging from the heavy persecution may have been one of the most important reasons the early Church remained as pure as it did until Constantine popularized Christianity. Saul's heart was never purged of the presence of another kingdom, his own. His own kingdom became more important to him than God's kingdom so he declared his own "holy war" to defend it.

David was made "fit for a king" by the unjust war that was waged against him. He humbled himself before the Lord and allowed the hand of God to both protect him and groom him for the future.

Again, Gene Edwards comments with clarity:

David the sheepherder would have grown up to become King Saul II, except God cut away the Saul inside David's heart. The operation, by the way, took years and was a brutalizing experience that almost killed the patient. And what were the scalpel and tongs God used to remove the inner Saul?

God used the outer Saul.

King Saul sought to destroy David, but his only success was that he became the handmaiden of God to put to death the Saul who roamed about in the caverns of David's own heart. Yes, it is true that David was virtually destroyed in the process, but this had to be. Otherwise the Saul in him would have survived.

Caves are not the ideal for morale building. There is a certain sameness to them all, no matter how many you have lived in. Dark. Wet. Cold. Stale. It is even worse when you are in them alone...and can hear the dogs baying.

But sometimes, when the dogs and hunters were not near, the prey sang. He started low, then lifted up his voice and sang the song the little lamb had taught him.

He sang a great deal.

There in those caves, drowned in the sorrow of his song, and in the song of his sorrow,

> David very simply became the greatest hymn
> writer, the greatest comforter of broken hearts
> this world shall ever know.[3]

God had made David "fit for a king."

FROM HEART EXPANSION
TO LIFE EXPRESSION

In Christ every Christian is a king and a priest unto God. Just as Jesus was a king who reigned in power, we are to reign in life through Christ Jesus. Just as Jesus was a priest who ministered with compassion and in humility, we are to humbly become debtors to all in need of His grace.

Instead of being kingdom builders, we need to be Kingdom bearers, bearing in our hearts the Kingdom of God. Our role as members of God's royal family is one in which His Kingdom is expressed through our lives. We are the material He uses to build the Kingdom.

Outward conflicts in "wineskin wars" reveal the inward conflicts that were never brought to Jesus for resolution. When Jesus is not king of our hearts, inner wars rage. Leaders whose inner conflicts are unresolved will start outer wars. Their claim will always be that they are justified because it is "holy war."

The "wineskin wars" under discussion cannot cease until "wineskin warriors" are converted to fight the real enemy. There is a war every king and priest is equipped to fight. It is time for a total disarmament of all carnal weaponry, time for a cease fire with each other declared.

There are some basic realities that must be remembered:

1. There is only room for one king to reign at a time. Our crowns must be placed at His feet daily. Though we reign as joint heirs, we never rule as joint Lord. He is Lord of lords.

2. There are no quick cures to guarantee success in the Kingdom of King Jesus. Instead, a childlike heart and a lifetime of growing in grace await us.

3. Those who win in the Kingdom are willing to lose. They will lose all and count it as waste to gain the excellency of the knowledge of God. No defense is needed because the willingness to lose is the means by which they win.

4. Those who rule in this Kingdom are those who serve the most. Towels for washing feet as a servant are standard equipment.

5. The strength of these leaders may be best judged by how much they cry. They cry as Jesus did over cities that need to come to safe shelter. They cry as Jesus did...for others and with others.

6. The weapons that are mighty through God are gifts on deposit from God. These gifts are standard issue for destroying the works of the devil. Gifts lift up Jesus so that others may see the incomparable one we are seeing.

Without Kingdom expansion in our hearts, we cannot have Kingdom expression from our lives. At the heart of Kingdom operatives is the condition of our hearts. Purity of heart is an essential element of Kingdom sightedness. Seeing God can only occur from a pure heart. Lenses of the heart that are pure can receive the image of God's outshining splendor.

These graphic accounts of the contrast between Saul and David are not insignificant. I believe the Lord recorded them to guide us to life in an unshakable Kingdom. Having right hearts and right weapons will enable us to fight the right battle.

Let's return to that account of a former battlefront.

LESSONS IN WARFARE

1. *Maintain Control of Your Weapons*

During the days when Saul was king, the Philistines (those who are controlled by the flesh and enemies of the spirit) actually controlled the sharpening of the Israelites' swords and spears. When the enemy controls the arsenal of weapons, it's a sign that few, if any, will be issued.

> *There were no blacksmiths in the land of Israel in those days. The Philistines wouldn't*

*allow them for fear they would make swords
and spears for the Hebrews. So whenever the
Israelites needed to sharpen their plowshares,
picks, axes, or sickles, they had to take them
to a Philistine blacksmith. (The schedule of
charges was as follows: a quarter of an ounce
of silver for sharpening a plowshare or a pick,
and an eighth of an ounce for sharpening an
ax, a sickle, or an ox goad.) So none of the
people of Israel had a sword or spear, except
for Saul and Jonathan* (1 Samuel 13:19-22
NLT).

We have allowed the enemy, the flesh, to control our weaponry. Our training systems of ministry are usually patterned after a secular model, not a spiritual, experiential model. We are more aware of theories than realities. People with an experience are often graded by people with a theory.

2. *Use Your Weapons*

Since only Saul and his son Jonathan could afford weapons of warfare, only two men in the army were properly equipped with weapons. When only two men have weapons and only one of them uses the weapon he carries, what chance of victory exists? Today few know they have weapons of warfare that are mighty through God. Fewer still are willing to use them.

3. *Don't Lay Down on the Job*

Jonathan, not Saul, was the only one willing to use his weapon. Saul carried the anointing of the Lord. He stood head and shoulders above other men. Yet instead of facing the enemies who were committed to destroying him and God's people, he was under the pomegranate tree in Migron (see 1 Sam. 14:2).

As Christians we are "the anointed ones"; that is part of the meaning of the name. But authority unused is no better than no authority at all. A tall man, like Saul, who's lying down is no better off than the shortest man in the camp.

Many today, who could stand head and shoulders above the world's best, are resting in passivity under the pomegranate trees. While they rest, the enemy goes on killing, stealing, and destroying.

4. The Lord Will Win With a Few

Jonathan dared to believe the Lord could win their battle so he said to his armor bearer, who is a picture of the Holy Spirit with us, *"Perhaps the Lord will help us, for nothing can hinder the Lord. He can win a battle whether he has many warriors or only a few"* (1 Sam. 14:6 NLT).

It has never been a majority, but a willing minority that the Lord has used to begin a breakthrough work.

5. Do All That the Lord Puts in the Heart

The armor bearer said to Jonathan, *"Do all that is in your heart. Go then; here I am with you, according to your heart"* (1 Sam. 14:7). If we listen to our heads, we may allow ourselves to be talked out of the things the Lord is telling us to do. It is the heart that houses God's orders. It is the heart that is to lead.

6. *Two May Be the Biggest Church in Town*

When Jonathan and the armor bearer approached the barracks of the Philistines, Jonathan said to the armor bearer, *"The Lord has delivered them into the hand of Israel"* (1 Sam. 14:12). He was seeing only two men as all of Israel. Out of the thousands who constituted Israel, only two were acting in covenant agreement with God. The rest remained under the pomegranate tree or in other places of self-protection while the two offered their lives by believing God. Sometimes the biggest church in town is where two or more are gathered in the presence of Jesus.

LESSONS IN LEADERSHIP

1. *Some Leaders Seek Image Above the People's Needs*

Saul was like many a leader who had to race to the front to appear to be leading. He heard that Jonathan and the armor bearer were winning the battle. As they fought, God sent an earthquake. Pandemonium broke out, and the Philistines fled before the presence of the three—Jonathan, the armor bearer, and the Lord. With the Lord on their side, only two people are a majority.

When Saul arrived, he did what leaders are trained to do, look like a leader. Without knowing all he should have known, he gave an order that contained an oath. He commanded that no one could eat until dark to ensure that all of the enemy was driven out (see 1 Sam. 14:24). His image was put above the needs of the people. His safety and security were his first consideration.

2. *God's Food Strengthens and Brightens the Eyes*

As Jonathan pursued the fleeing Philistines, he passed through a forest and found honey on the ground. Not knowing his father's edict, he stretched out his rod and took the honey. Immediately, strength came into his body and his eyes brightened (see 1 Sam. 14:27). Honey contains the purest form of energy of any food. God's word is *"sweeter than honey and the honeycomb"* (Ps. 19:10). Jonathan's brightened eyes and strengthened body prepared him for a much greater victory.

3. *"Deaf" Leaders Will "Trouble" the Land*

When Jonathan realized the oath his father had made, refusing to let people eat and gain strength, this is how he responded:

> *"My father has made trouble for us all!" Jonathan exclaimed. "A command like that only hurts us. See how much better I feel now that I have eaten this little bit of honey. If the men had been allowed to eat freely from the food they found among our enemies, think how many more Philistines we could have killed"* (1 Samuel 14:29-30 NLT).

Church fathers and church leaders often tell people not to eat the food the Lord has provided. Strength and bright eyes are threatening to the insecure leader who is victimized by the fear of men. When leader's eyes still contain the scales of fleshly conformity, the people will be deprived of the strength they need for the fight.

4. Starving People Eat the Wrong Things

Because the people fought all day without food, they were famished. Hunger gripped them. Acute fatigue so drained them that when they found animals, they ate them, blood and all. Dietary practices for good health were violated.

No wonder people today eat spiritual junk food or whatever they can get to bring some temporary satisfaction to a ravenous appetite. Insecure leaders often caution people against attending conferences marked by the presence of God. Warnings about excesses become so loud that people are left without the abundance they deserve for fear of an excess. It is like a person going to a lovely swimming pool to enjoy the cool water and hearing a lifeguard reviewing for them all the pool regulations and the dangers of diving. Both the high dive and the low diving board have their dangers. Instead of the lifeguard demonstrating the dives and exhibiting the enjoyment of being in the water, they leave the would-be swimmers so afraid they decide to leave the pool without going in the water. Such leaders are usually more concerned about their own security than the welfare of the people. Saul was such a leader. Forbidding to eat can lead people to eat the wrong thing and often far too much of the wrong thing.

5. Pride Can Make a Leader Destroy the People

Saul had pronounced an oath. Jonathan had violated it. *"Saul said to Jonathan, 'Tell me what you have done?' And Jonathan...said, 'I only tasted a little honey with the end of the rod that was in my hand. So now I must die'"* (1 Sam. 14:43).

The people interceded for Jonathan. Saul's pride would not have stopped until he had killed his own son. Instead of acknowledging who had really been the Lord's instrument to win the battle, he planned to kill the one who was instrumental in saving his own life. Many sons of ministries, whose leaders do not have hearts filled with God's heart, have been sacrificed in the name of "ruling in order to look good."

George Whitefield was used by God in the First Great Awakening, which in many senses birthed America from colony status into an independent nation. But Whitefield was considered an embarrassment by those who ordained him. It's amazing how many we have killed or stifled because of blinding pride or threats to our own little ministry territory.

A BATTLE SUMMARY

We have the weapons of warfare that God has forged for us. Our weapons are mighty through God to the pulling down of strongholds.

The enemy's favorite tactic today is to lead us to ignore both the battle and the "smart weapons" that belong to us. Our enemy is never our brother or our sister.

> *For we are not fighting against people made of flesh and blood, but against persons without bodies—the evil rulers of the unseen world, those mighty satanic beings and great evil princes of darkness who rule this world; and against huge numbers of wicked spirits in the spirit world* (Ephesians 6:12 TLB).

We fight a battle that is already won. We declare the victory won in the cross and resurrection of Jesus. On the one hand, the Church is in need of a makeover more than most of us have been willing to acknowledge. On the other hand, it is not beyond restoration, either. There is nothing broken that God can't fix. God's ability to restore has been demonstrated again and again.

Wineskin wars are not necessary. They are fought with weapons aimed at the wrong target. But they can end with tolerance for viewpoints or practices different from ours. Forgiveness of wrongs inflicted in these wars will occur as we chose to forgive those who sin against us. His Kingdom can come. His will can be done on earth as it is in Heaven.

Chapter 8

WHO'S WHO IN THE KINGDOM

SEEING CHRIST IN US

Who Christ is in us and who we are in Christ are the two most important realities of the Kingdom. Christ is in us. We are in Him. He is never on leave of absence from being in us. We are never quarantined or exiled away from Him.

God taking up residence on earth in the body of Jesus Christ is the centerpiece of Scripture. That is further extended because Christ has entered every believer as the resident companion of life. Christ in us is the hope of glory (see Col. 1:27). The eternal, unchanging Christ takes up residency in our lives. We are no less inhabited by Him than was Mary. In fact, we are more inhabited because His life mission on earth is complete and His habitation in us is for more than nine months.

Christ in us is the eternal purpose of God being fulfilled by His incarnation being extended beyond one life to every life willing to receive this gift of God. Mary had to decide if she would open her life to receive His life in her. So do we. This treasure of Heaven in us makes our lives clay pots housing His infinite worth (see 2 Cor. 4:7). But we are not only called clay pots by the one who knows us best; we are also called temples of the Holy Presence (see 1 Cor. 3:16). This treasure, this presence, is the unchanging Christ.

Perfection does not need change, nor can it be changed for the better. Christ, in His incomparable role of God in a human life, is perfect. He is God on display. People were offered the privilege of seeing God the Father by seeing Him. The same offering included seeing the Kingdom because with Him the Kingdom was present.

In his classic book *The Unshakeable Kingdom and the Unchanging Person,* E. Stanley Jones offers a clear view of the eternal qualities of Christ and the permanency of the Kingdom:

> The rediscovery of Jesus without the rediscovery of the kingdom of God would be a half-discovery—a king without a kingdom, a lone figure unrelated. But a rediscovery of the Kingdom without the rediscovery of the King would also be a half discovery, for it would be a kingdom without a king. But since it is a kingdom of God and a kingdom among men, then only the God-Man could be the illustration of its meaning. Jesus shows us what God is like and also shows us what the kingdom

of God is like in operation. The kingdom of
God is Christlikeness universalized.[1]

With a clear understanding of Jesus, His Kingdom, and
how it relates to us, E. Stanley Jones further said,

> God chose...a disguised form...the Babe, the
> Boy, the Carpenter, the Prophet, the Son of
> man, the Son of God, the Redeemer, the Cru-
> cified, the risen and alive Redeemer, the One
> who sat at the right hand of ultimate power in
> the universe—thus He revealed the Kingdom
> in a Person.
>
> Would men take that kingdom in such a
> form? Some did and were transformed and
> showed a quality of life and power far beyond
> the ordinary. But the many did not, and as a
> consequence lived half-lives by half-lights, or
> fumbled and stumbled in the dark.[2]

Living half-lives by half-lights with stumbling steps is
not what the Scripture describes as the normal Christian
life. Kingdom-sightedness enables us to see life as the master
designer intended it. E. Stanley Jones concluded that everyone is
seeking the Kingdom; they just don't know it. He further concluded that when the day comes that people see the Kingdom,
we will have the greatest spiritual awakening this planet has
ever seen. Who Christ is defines the Kingdom. Who Christ is
also defines us.

God was in Christ reconciling the world unto Himself. Christ is in us with the same Kingdom purpose to be experienced and extended. Having walked the battlelines of conflict in the previous two chapters on warfare, I want to emphasize an essential element in winning the spiritual war that rages currently. Many of the personal defeats as well as the corporate defeats of Church life today grow out of our lack of knowing who we are in Christ. So my emphasis in this "who's who of the Kingdom" is going to be focused on us more than on Christ.

My reason is based on the perception that we have a better grasp of who Christ is than we do of who we are in Him. Our determined enemy is unchanged, just as our Champion in the spiritual battle is unchanged. So, gaining intelligence reports on the enemy is helpful. Military tactics and strategies found in Scripture have value. Demonic activity was unquestioned by the early church. They not only knew they had a fight on their hands, but also knew how to win it.

"BUT WHO ARE YOU?"

When seven men were asked the question "But who are you?" by a demon, they had no answer. Without an answer, they fled, stripped naked, wounded, and afraid. Many Christians today feel that same nakedness and fear when challenged by a diabolical enemy.

Those seven brothers were challenged by a demon because the brothers commendably sought to offer freedom to a person in bondage. This account is a significant intelligence report:

A team of itinerant Jews who were travel-
ing from town to town casting out demons
planned to experiment by using the name of
the Lord Jesus. The incantation they decided
on was this: "I adjure you by Jesus, whom Paul
preaches, to come out!" Seven sons of Sceva, a
Jewish priest, were doing this. But when they
tried it on a man possessed by a demon, the
demon replied, "I know Jesus and I know
Paul, but who are you?" And he leaped on
two of them and beat them up, so that they
fled out of his house naked and badly injured
(Acts 19:13-16 TLB).

They couldn't answer the question "But who are you?"
because they weren't Christians. Many Christians today have
a relationship with Christ, but can't answer the question any
better than these brothers. Instead of standing strong in Christ,
they flee in defeat. The demon knew who Christ is and said so.
Because Paul was in Christ and Christ was in him, the demon
knew Paul. "But who are you?" meant the demon did not recognize these brothers as a part of God's family with Kingdom
rights.

Jesus faced the same questions about His identity. His
showdown with satan began with the question of identity. *"If*
you be the son of God," was the preface to the first two temp-
tations (see Matt. 4:3). Jesus knew who He was and was not
seeking to create an identity. His identity was well established.
The third temptation was a temptation related to His establishment of a kingdom. He was offered a kingdom forfeited

by Adam. He refused that tarnished kingdom in favor of the worship of God, whose Kingdom He brought with him. At the centerpiece of that Kingdom is worship in Spirit and in truth.

Security in His identity allowed Jesus to ask the disciples who others thought He was. The answers could have discouraged Him, had He not known His identity was already established by the Father who said, *"You are My beloved son in whom I am well pleased"* (Luke 3:22). The people's most common descriptions identified Him as one of the prophets from the past. The disciples could have reported that some were saying He was a drunkard or even a devil. From the cross, Jesus heard the same accusations about His identity. *"If you are the son of God, come down from the cross and save yourself"* (Matt. 27:40).

This final assault about His identity occurred when He was exchanging His identity with us. He was being made sin for us though He had no sin. His own identity would be exchanged with us so ours could be found in Him. First He had to take our identity so we could take His identity as our own. Jesus was willing to be made sin, knowing it would cost Him the identity He had known eternally. He also knew that His eternal identity and that identity alone could destroy sin. *"Behold the Lamb of God who takes away the sin of the world"* (John 1:29) resonated in His heart. John had announced him publicly because he knew who He was and what He came to do. He was the Lamb of God, eternal and spotless, and He would absorb sin in His spotless life. Everything He did was done because He knew who He was. His father told him, *"You are my beloved son"* and He believed Him.

Our problem in answering the question, "Who are you?" is usually the issue that most needs to be settled. Either we have never heard the Father tell us who we are, or we have heard and thought it was too good to be true, or we have heard and then forgotten what we heard.

HEARING HEAVEN'S REPORT

God spoke from Heaven into the lives of missionaries in China. From that word He spoke again to me about my identity. From the life of Bertha Smith, missionary to China, came a challenge about my identity. With clear, piercing blue eyes she studied our faces and asked, "Whatever led you to believe you are a saved sinner?" She further challenged, "Show me that in Scripture!" Then she drove home this truth, "You can't be saved and a sinner. If you are saved, the Bible declares you are a saint."

From childhood, I was taught two kinds of people populate planet earth, "saved sinners and lost sinners." The teaching said further that it is the job of saved sinners to lead lost sinners into the saved sinner category. Bertha Smith's words shook my theological structure. Though I heard her words, words that came from Heaven, I did not embrace them. They were good words, but the music from the reality of them was not playing in my heart.

That would change in the atmosphere of better hearing at Graceland in 1980. Suddenly, the words spoken in my heart on the plane in route to Graceland came alive,

> *I will hear what the Lord will speak, for He will speak peace to His people...mercy and truth have met together; righteousness and peace have kissed* (Psalm 85:8,10).

God wasn't saying what I was expecting. I was hearing from Heaven. My choice of words was not His. I wanted Him to speak "repentance" to His people. He was speaking peace. He was connecting the affection of righteousness and peace kissing to something I needed to understand. I did understand that I did not understand, so that was a starting point.

THE REIGNING RIGHTS OF RIGHTEOUSNESS

Quoted verses do not constitute known verses. One of the false conclusions that comes from being able to quote a Bible verse is the assumption we know the verse. I knew the verse in Psalm 85:10, that righteousness and peace kiss each other, yet on that plane I realized I only knew the words, not the meaning. Another verse I knew well was Romans 5:17:

> *For if by one man's offence death reigned through the one; much more those who receive abundance of grace and of the gift of righteousness will reign in life through the one, Jesus Christ.*

With the quickening of the thought about righteousness, I began to examine every verse I knew that related to righteousness.

The Book of Romans was my "Bethel" because I was preaching through it in 1966 when God visited us in First Baptist Church, West Plains, Missouri. I had written a book on Chapters 5 through 8, the heart of this incomparable epistle. Now a verse I thought I knew contained a thought I had never considered. In receiving what Romans 5:17 was saying, I saw that those who *"receive the gift of righteousness will reign in life."* After being a Christian for over 30 years, I stood face-to-face with this verse as if for the first time, and concluded that I had never received the gift of righteousness. It was mine in Christ, but it was not mine in understanding or, more importantly, in appropriation.

My mind raced on for further verification in other passages. One I could quickly recall was John 16:7-11. There Jesus described the Holy Spirit showing us sin, righteousness, and judgment. He said righteousness would belong to us because He would go to the Father and not be seen visibly. That fit with the fact that He is ever taking our case to the Father.

> *My dear children, I write this to you so that you will not sin. But if anybody does sin, we have one who speaks to the Father in our defense—Jesus Christ, the Righteous One* (1 John 2:1-2 NIV).

It was in that awakened state of mind that I realized that not only was I not a "saved sinner," I was actually a new creation in Christ and appeared to God always in the clothing of Christ's righteousness. Just as Abraham believed God and it was counted righteous, I would not achieve righteousness by my performance. I would receive righteousness by my faith. As I had received Christ by faith for my salvation, I received Christ's righteousness as my standing before God and before the spirit world. For the first time in my life the melody of those words was heard in my heart; I was the righteousness of God in Christ (see 2 Cor. 5:21). By faith based on Christ's completed work, I could say, "I am a Christian." By faith based on Christ's perfect life shared with me, I could say, "I am the righteousness of God through Christ."

It was then I understood why righteousness and peace kiss each other. I realized that was the order of the armor in Ephesians chapter 6. As we put on the whole armor of God, we start with truth. Truth leads us to put on the breastplate of righteousness. That covering of righteousness is followed with peace covering our feet. Again I saw this truth in the James 3:18: *"And the fruit of righteousness is sown in peace by those who make peace."* Peace is not sustainable without a righteousness consciousness. The enemy comes as an accuser to bring charges against us. Understanding our righteous identity with God allows us to know the peace of God. Peace covers our feet and allows us to walk with comfort. No wonder we are often immobile in moving to touch the lives of others. We are foot weary instead of having "happy feet" covered in peace.

Later in my life's journey, the Lord used an exchange of clothes to drive home to me the reality of Jesus being my righteousness. A wealthy friend whose professional life called for impeccable dress was the same size as I am. He bought his Oxford suits at Neiman Marcus in Dallas, 10 to 15 at time. They are virtually indestructible, so every five years or so he would purchase a new supply and give me the former ones. (He now wears even better clothes in Heaven.) His suits and sport coats are still the basic clothes of my wardrobe.

The suits that filled my closet cost $2,000 to $3,000 each. My penny-pinching approach would never have allowed me to pay that much money or have that many suits. Though I could not have afforded them, I wear them with pleasure because of my love for him and the honor of wearing something of quality he wanted me to have.

I was reminded by the Lord that I had always been dressed in clothes that I could not afford. Being clothed in the righteousness of Christ has similarity to wearing the clothes of my friend. Fine-tailored clothes fit so well and feel so good. Such is the righteousness of Christ. It fits so well and feels so good.

Reigning in life comes when righteousness is received as a grace gift. Without reigning rights, Kingdom rights are not practiced. *"For the kingdom of God is not eating and drinking, but righteousness, peace and joy in the Holy Spirit"* (Rom. 14:17).

WHO WE ARE DETERMINES WHAT WE DO

Immaturity and dysfunctional behavior on the part of Christians is a direct result of being void of a righteousness consciousness. Skill in the word of righteousness is essential for skills in Kingdom engagements.

> *Anyone who lives on milk, being still an infant, is not acquainted with the teaching about righteousness. But solid food is for the mature, who by constant use have trained themselves to distinguish good from evil* (Hebrews 5:13-14 NIV).

If we do not know that the gift of righteousness is ours, we suffer from acute amnesia. In that vacuum of understanding, we can't distinguish good from evil. If good and evil are indiscernible, then simple choices on important or unimportant matters are even less clear. We have a high level of incompetency because we simply don't know what to do. Who I am and why I am here are companions of identity.

Robert Lewis in his book, *The Church of Irresistible Influence,* points out how the Church may succeed by cultural standards, but not have real significance.[3] Impacted by the book *Half Time,* as well as the friendship of Bob Buford, the author, Lewis evaluated the church he pastored.[4] Bob Buford suggested that often success is measured by financial strength and the ability to buy "grown-up toys." Many people excel in a system set by a traditional standard and feel successful. But true significance is a standard set by the Lord that is relevant today, reaches to all in our area or city, and has eternal consequences. For me, that is another way of saying "significance" is a Kingdom experience that is enacted with an effect on others, both now and eternally.

Facing the same possibilities of being successful in church life and yet not significant in impacting the neighborhood, the city, and the culture around him, Robert Lewis courageously called for a church to rethink its mission. Such humility and insightfulness is the epitome of Kingdom-mindedness. Out of that Kingdom-awareness, Church life throughout Little Rock, Arkansas, was enhanced.

We are at a critical point in our culture in America. Never has there been a greater opportunity for Kingdom life to be demonstrated, nor has there been a greater need. How we see ourselves always regulates how we treat others. Loving our neighbors comes out of loving ourselves. Jesus made that clear.

When we have low self-esteem, we have low value for those for whom Christ gave His life.

Our value is seen by Christ's payment for us in His life and death. We are His purchased possession. That establishes our worth. But the worth of every person is established through that price. There are no worthless people. All individuals have Christ's proportionate value attached to them through His love.

MIRROR, MIRROR ON THE WALL...

The evil queen's question in the Disney classic *Snow White* is at the heart of this issue of our identity: "Mirror, mirror on the wall, who's the fairest of them all?" We seek the aid of a mirror to check on our appearance. Our reason for consulting the mirror is to see if we have put ourselves together properly to venture beyond the family circle.

Until the word of righteousness was spoken to my heart, my own concept of the mirror in James was negative. I would read,

> *Anyone who listens to the word but does not do what it says is like a man who looks at his face in a mirror and, after looking at himself, goes away and immediately forgets what he looks like* (James 1:23-24 NIV).

Without consciously doing it, I had become a "transposer" of Scripture in the way a musician transposes a melody. I shifted it to a negative key. So, it read *"...is like a man who looks at his face in a mirror and, after looking at himself, goes away and immediately forgets* [how bad] *he looks."* Then one day as I read it, it read me. Suddenly I realized that we forget how *good* we look, not how bad we look.

This mirror on the wall is God's Word. We see ourselves in it, and even though we find that when our hair is messed up or our collar is stained, we still look good. We look good enough to comb our hair and remove the stain, good enough to appear in Christ and walk to our engagement, knowing that His record of our righteousness stands, good enough to know there is *"now no condemnation to those in Christ"* (Rom. 8:1).

The most frustrating chapter in the Bible for me was Romans 7. I had written a devotional commentary on it and did the intellectually dishonest thing. Due to the publisher's deadline, I submitted it without knowing the meaning of some verses. I knew that whatever Paul knew when he wrote, *"...it is no longer I who do it, but sin..."* (Rom. 7:20), I didn't know. I fussed with Paul. "If it wasn't you that sinned, then who was it?" Years after the book was published, I got it. Paul knew who he was in Christ. He knew that sin was not an extension of him, but a contradiction of him. Sin was not him, but a dead man tied to him that could be removed if he asked for help in the right way. He could ask, "Who will deliver me?" not, "What will deliver me?" (See Romans 7:24.) Then he saw Christ and thanked God for His removal of this awful, grotesque contradiction of who he was.

Because he had stood in front of the mirror and knew who he was, he did not cave in under the weight of the sin he found so repulsive. God grants repentance because His goodness shows us our sins for what they are and shows us that our sins are not us. Hannah Whitall Smith plumbed the depths of this issue in the book *The Christian's Secret of a Happy Life.*[5] She said that if sin is us, rather than a contradiction of us, we would be like the person with a terrible headache. Only two alternatives would exist. Get rid of the head or put up with the headache. People know they can ill afford to be without a head, so they put up with the headache. But if sin is not us, we can get rid of the headache and keep our head.

Getting rid of sin is a major Kingdom issue. The preparation for Jesus to walk into the spotlight of people's attention called for *"Repent for the Kingdom of God is at hand"* (Matt. 3:2). Repentance comes because the goodness of God leads to repentance (see Rom. 2:4). When we see who God sees when He sees us, His goodness leads us to repentance. His picture of us is found in the mirror of His Word. This self image is a transforming image.

Kingdom exploits can be done when people check their appearance in the mirror before going out to the engagements of life. This was really brought home to me a few years ago in a retreat.

The speaker asked, "Do you know why God would not let Moses grow up with the people he was going to lead from 400 years of captivity?" Well, I didn't know, but I was sure he would tell us.

Sure enough, he said, "He couldn't live among his own people, who were slaves, without thinking like a slave. He needed to live among royalty to think like a king. So God in his wisdom chose for him to live as royalty and think as royalty so he could lead slaves to freedom." Slave mentality cannot impact the culture we are part of. We must think like

Kingdom citizens. We are members of His royal family with the mind of Christ ruling our minds.

Who we are in Christ is more than "saved sinners." We are new creations created in perfection by the mighty hand of God to take up Kingdom positions of significance. We came to the Kingdom for such a time as this. We came with God's DNA as the genetic blueprint of our lives. We are members of royalty and need to think like royalty, act like royalty, and speak like royalty. A royal decree has been made that is irrevocable: we are kings and priests, queens and priestesses before God. Now let's enjoy being who God made us to be.

Yes, that really is you in the mirror of His Word.

Chapter 9

THE GOSPEL WITH
AN ATTITUDE

Often people with "an attitude" are thought of in a negative way. However, attitudes can be positive, too. Our position on the positive or negative pole is always determined by our choice. The Gospel is always pegged out on the positive, but an attitude exists.

Part of the confusion with who we are, what we are doing here, and what we are to tell others comes from the confusion of newscasts that we are hearing and repeating. The Gospel is the newscast from Heaven to offer hope to everyone. This newscast is a broad-cast. We often hear a narrow-cast, and even worse, we transmit the narrow version. Many times the Gospel that Jesus proclaimed is preempted. The Gospel Paul learned from Jesus is often drowned out by another pop station stepping on that frequency. A not-so-golden-oldie station could be broadcasting from the wrong side of the finished work of Christ at the cross, calling for us to do our works for Christ. Or a message about how to feel good about ourselves may omit our identification in the cross altogether.

Gospel means good news. What was the news Jesus announced? More at issue, are we saying what He says?

JESUS IS THE CENTERPIECE OF THE GOSPEL

The centerpiece of history, Jesus Christ, is the centerpiece of the Gospel. The Gospel is not about Jesus; the Gospel is Jesus. Declaration did not create Jesus, who always was and always will be. Clothed in a body that was like a time capsule, He came here for 33 years. Out of an eternal timelessness, there was a very short timeline of 33 years that He spent in a human body.

Christ is first and last, beginning and end, and everything in between. Paul knew this and said it more succinctly—*"He is all and in all"* (Col. 3:11). When God was everything because nothing else existed, He started His creative masterpiece using Christ as the creative Word. *In the beginning was the Word—* the Christ-Word (see John 1:1). At the end, Christ will be the great presider who will gavel history's conclusion. This One, who is the light of the world, will turn out the lights of this world in the timed event we call life. He will pull the curtain on time and declare that the eternity of His existence has been extended to all who know Him.

With perfection He lived here and died here so we could enter Him and He could enter us. That double entry connects us to His eternal being. A stake was driven in history to announce a completed work. That stake was His cross. The offense of the cross is the fact that our sin necessitated it. It is sin that we commit out of our free will, but that only He can wipe off the record. Our offense comes out of our proud nature, not wanting to admit that everything rests solely on Him and in Him.

"At the cross, at the cross where I first saw the light"[1] was the first sight I got of Jesus. When I first saw Him die for me as a nine-year-old boy, I was offended. He was offering Himself to me, and I exercised the very will He had granted me to choose against Him. That choice stood until I was 16. Then I invited Him to enter my life, and the evidence of that was peace with God.

THE GOSPEL JESUS DECLARED

When Jesus declared the Gospel, He declared the Kingdom.

> ...*Jesus came to Galilee, preaching the gospel of the kingdom of God, and saying, "The time is fulfilled, and the kingdom of God is at hand. Repent, and believe in the gospel"* (Mark 1:14-15).

His presence carried with Him the operative Kingdom. The manifest presence of God is an enactment of God's presence that enhances His omnipresence. He is always present because He is God. This increase or manifested presence is

God announcing Himself as present. God bears witness to His presence as if taking the microphone and declaring, "I am here."

Jesus was announcing the good news as His presence manifested, with the attending enactments of His Kingdom. All the manifestations of His presence we have optioned to call "revival"; He called them Kingdom operatives.

PAUL'S ACQUAINTANCE WITH THE GOSPEL

Paul knew the Gospel and defined the Gospel as no one else other than Jesus. He learned it from Jesus. His introduction to the Gospel came directly from Jesus. It was not a set of facts presented with logic, clarity, and persuasiveness that introduced Paul to Jesus Christ. When deciding who would declare His life and presence to Paul, Jesus chose Himself.

> *Meanwhile, Saul was still breathing out murderous threats against the Lord's disciples. He went to the high priest and asked him for letters to the synagogues in Damascus, so that if he found any there who belonged to the Way, whether men or women, he might take them as prisoners to Jerusalem. As he neared Damascus on his journey, suddenly a light from heaven flashed around him. He fell to the ground and heard a voice say to him, "Saul, Saul, why do you persecute Me?" "Who are you, Lord?" Saul asked. "I am Jesus, whom you are persecuting,"* He replied... (Acts 9:1-6 NIV).

That encounter with Jesus was a transforming experience. Christ was formed in Paul. And Paul was immediately in Christ and could write later on, with supernatural guidance, *"If anyone is in Christ he is a new creation"* (2 Cor. 5:17). He knew Christ was in him, and his own life was hidden with Christ in God.

With Christ as His teacher, He came to know Him and His Kingdom as no one else. The presence of Christ was His teacher. He did not counsel with men, but went into isolation in Arabia for a lengthy period (see Gal. 1:15-18).

Good news was His message. He was unashamed of this good news because it was the *"power of God unto salvation"* (Rom. 1:16). At the center of the Gospel He knew was the same centerpiece of Christ's presence. His definition of the good news was the "power of God" (see Rom. 1:16; 1 Cor. 2:4). The power of God was residing in the One to whom all power and authority belongs, in Heaven and on earth—namely, Jesus.

Paul knew that Jesus Christ was the Gospel, and he equally knew that Kingdom engagements were part of Jesus' presence. He could not separate Jesus from the Gospel nor could he separate the Kingdom from Jesus. Good news came to Paul in Christ Himself. Christ's Kingdom came to him in the person of Christ.

As Paul departed Ephesus, knowing that imprisonment was near, he reviewed his teaching: *"And indeed, now I know that you all, among whom I have gone **preaching the kingdom of God,** will see my face no more"* (Acts 20:25).

These passages from Acts also provide capsulated accounts of his focus:

...From morning till evening he explained and declared to them the kingdom of God and tried to convince them about Jesus from the Law of Moses and from the Prophets (Acts 28:23 NIV).

Preaching the kingdom of God and teaching the things which concern the Lord Jesus Christ with all confidence, no one forbidding him (Acts 28:31).

Paul so valued the Gospel he received from Jesus that he stood for it without compromise. He declared that anyone who alters this Gospel of good news will be *"accursed"* (see Gal. 1:8). Further he declared that the church at Galatia had been *"bewitched"* or duped by demon spirits into altering the Gospel (see Gal. 3:1). The Judaizers who tried to mix an old system of religion into the perfected work of Christ were slipping something into the drinks of the Galatians. They were deceived. In their blending of Jesus with their own best efforts, they had fallen from grace. Grace was operative, but they fell below the benefits of it. No longer was the Gospel being shared at Galatia. The Gospel was Christ plus nothing. But they taught Christ plus their religious additives and best efforts.

This compelling Gospel that Paul championed was more than the content of facts. His Gospel was not only the truth about the person and finished work of Christ, but was also the presence of Christ, who was there to speak for Himself. He knew that Christ came and spoke for Himself to him. It was this dependency that caused him, after 27 years of knowing

Him, to say, *"That I may know Him in the power of His resur-rection, and the fellowship of His sufferings, being conformed to His death"* (Phil. 3:10).

He declared the presence of Christ in the Gospel in this way.

> *My message and my preaching were not with wise and persuasive words, but with a dem-onstration of the Spirit's power, so that your faith might not rest on men's wisdom, but on God's power* (1 Corinthians 2:4-5 NIV).

Life and death hang on the issue of the Gospel. Paul was unrelenting as the Spirit compelled him to pursue the issues. He cautioned the Corinthian church that another Jesus could be presented, not the eternal Jesus who lived at Nazareth.

> *But I fear, lest somehow, as the serpent deceived Eve by his craftiness, so your minds may be corrupted from the simplicity that is in Christ. For if he who comes preaches another Jesus whom we have not preached, or if you receive a different spirit which you have not received, or a different gospel which you have not accepted—you may well put up with it* (2 Corinthians 11:3-4).

Another Jesus, another spirit, and another Gospel com-pound the corruption. Getting the Gospel right cannot take place apart from Christ. We must see that the presence of

Christ embodies the Gospel, as well as the true facts about Him. The facts about His perfect life, His death to pay for our sin, and His return to life in the resurrection victory are important. Never can they be discounted. We can declare Him. But we cannot re-present Him. Only He can present Himself. The content of the Gospel is important. The person of the Gospel is essential.

WHEN JESUS COMES CALLING

In countries around the world there are numerous accounts of Muslims experiencing Jesus coming to them in the night in dreams or visions. "Campus Crusade for Christ has received thousands of letters from Muslims, many of whom claim to have had a similar dream of Christ, according to the ministry's radio broadcast office in northern Africa. In the dream, Jesus appears and tells people, "I am the way," Campus Crusade founder and president Bill Bright said. Moved by the dreams, they contact the radio ministry and "freely respond" to the gospel message, he said. In Algeria, an imprisoned Muslim political radical said Jesus appeared to her in her cell. The woman now is a Christian and works with Campus Crusade ministering to Muslims."[1]

Out of that awareness of His presence, they are converted to Him.

Jesus chose the same approach to Paul. He went personally, without a human instrument. My own theory as to why is simple. I don't think He could find anyone who was willing to write his own death warrant by sharing the Gospel with Paul. Stephen died seeing Jesus because Paul acted as an instigator. He stood in the shadows holding the coats of the attackers (see Acts 7:58). Who was ready and willing to go to this number-one enemy of every Christian? I think that because no one was willing to be the witness to this unrelenting killer, Jesus went Himself.

I also think that is why, in the Muslim world, Jesus often does it Himself. We are so inept at relating to people who may hate us or whose commitment to their religious beliefs is as great or greater than our commitment to Christ. Thus, Jesus must do it Himself. Without His perfect love, which casts out fear and leads us to serve our way into being heard, we are inept in reaching Muslims.

One of the reasons for my conclusion comes out of an experience I had in the days of God's visitation in West Plains, Missouri. Our neighbor to the north was a wonderful person. His wife and daughter were members of the church where I served. Les was an easy man to have lawn and driveway conversations with. Many times I shared my appreciation for him and how his greatest need and deepest satisfaction would be in knowing Christ in his own life. He was polite, but uninterested.

As the Lord's presence was being declared in countless ways and even reported in the *West Plains Daily Quill* with the headline, "God Is Alive," Les, like most people in the region, knew something unusual was occurring. Occasionally he would attend church, but he didn't come during those days of the Lord's visitation. I prayed for an opening to talk with him in his coming or going in the driveway. But it never occurred.

Suddenly, I was awakened one Sunday morning thinking about Les. It was three in the morning. I got up and began praying for him. There was such an urgency that I heard the Lord tell me to go and knock on his door. This was all new to me, and my ability to walk in the Spirit was limited. I was walking on very unsteady legs. I thought, *Lord, I may be losing my mind! I just can't go knock on his door at 3:00 A.M. Have him turn on a light so I know he is up.*

I looked out our window toward their house, and it looked like a light was on in the house. I dressed and went out the back door into our drive. There I realized that I had seen the reflection of a street light on their window. It was not a light in their house, but simply reflected light. Without saying a word to the Lord, I wheeled and went back to our house and tried to get a little sleep.

In the church service a few hours later, I sat on the platform and saw a packed building with extra chairs. My eyes searched for one man. I found his wife and daughter in the balcony, but he was not there. My heart sank. It was deer-hunting season, and I knew he was an ardent hunter. *What if he is killed in the deer woods and I live with this lack of obedience all my life?* I thought.

At the end of the service, as his wife went out, I stopped her and asked about Les. She said, "He never came to bed last night, but sat in the living room and then left early to go to the deer woods. I have never seen him like this. I think the Lord is really drawing him." Then I knew that he was sitting there in his living room and that I could and should have gone, even at 3:00 A.M. I was late getting home from church, and as I drove in our drive way Les drove into his. I got out of my car and started toward him, but found he had already started toward me. His face was beaming. He said, "I took the Lord into my life this morning in the deer woods!" I buried him in my arms and rejoiced with him.

I could have been in on that joyous and life-changing experience in the life of Les Holloway, but I was not able to walk with total trust in the Lord's leading. Instead the Lord did it Himself, without me.

Normally, the Lord's presence will accompany the witness of those who are sharing their faith, but when we are not willing or not equipped, He does it without us. His presence through others is just as real as when He came personally to Paul, to the Muslim, or to Les Holloway.

Presence evangelism is the most impacting experience in evangelism. That is the dimension that I have witnessed in the visitations of His presence in some of the accounts I am sharing. Our witness of Him should not be silenced in the anticipation of a greater witness—His presence. But our anticipation of this witness of Himself should encourage us to be bolder and more confident in verbalizing who He is.

When I am listening to teaching or preaching, the question is always, is Jesus here in life-exchanging presence? When I am in a church service, I am asking, is Jesus here in declarative presence? If He is not there in the teaching or preaching, it is news, but it is not good news. Good news is His presence. If He is not there in declarative presence, I do not believe it is church, but a religious service. Church is not Church unless He can say, "This is my promise fulfilled: *I will build My church...*'" (Matt. 16:18). Only He can build His Church so that it becomes His Body, housing Him.

THE ATTITUDE OF THE GOSPEL

Everything Jesus did was based on knowing who He was and what He was here for. *"I must be about My Father's business"* (Luke 2:49) was clear to Him when He was only 12. His

Father's business was opened to customers when He heard from the Father, *"You are My beloved Son, and I am very pleased with you"* (Luke 3:22).

When Jesus went to John the Baptist for baptism, an act of fulfilling all righteousness, Heaven opened and the Holy Spirit came and rested on Him. It was then that the Father endowed Him with the anointing for opening the biggest business ever opened, the Kingdom of God (see Luke 4:18-19).

Soon in His own home town synagogue, He declared,

> *The Spirit of the Lord is upon Me because He has anointed Me to preach the gospel to the poor, heal the broken hearted, preach deliverance to the captives, recover sight for the blind, grant liberty to the wounded and proclaim the year of the Lord's provisions* (Luke 4:18-19).

That stated business plan of His Father had been published for 700 years, since it was originally declared by Isaiah (see Isa. 61:1-3). When Jesus stood up with those words, He was declaring, "Today we are opening, and this is our inventory. There is good news for those who are too poor to pay, healing for broken hearts, deliverance for those in spiritual bondage, sight for blindness, recovery for the decimated and addicted, and a warehouse of provisions for every need to be met out of the unlimited supply."

Jesus knew the business. He knew the inventory. He knew the value of everything. It was His business to do the Father's business, and that was announced in His grand opening statement, *"The kingdom is at hand"* (see Matt. 4:17).

When He declared, *"The kingdom is at hand,"* He was saying, "This is a mobile business. We will come where you are. House calls are made and deliveries are without charge." Church as most of us have known it is something you go to. The Kingdom comes to us and to others through us.

After setting the stage for His business, Jesus began training others to be part of this mobile business. His choices were based on the fact that He does not call the equipped, but He always equips the called. A ragged bunch of future store managers began their in-service training.

He took them on a retreat. A mountain side was a great place to start the training. The only problem was that the business was so exciting that the crowd was larger than if a pre-Christmas sale was on. Thousands were there with them. Everyone on that mountain was a potential customer, but amazingly enough, they were also potential store managers. The Kingdom enterprise would be big enough to require far more than a mountain full of people. A part of the Kingdom provision was a free lunch. Everyone on that mountain was a potential Kingdom person.

In the "street language" of The Message, I am taking space to include what today we call the "beatitudes." Jesus took both time and space to lay this essential foundation:

> *When Jesus saw His ministry drawing huge crowds, He climbed a hillside. Those who were apprenticed to Him, the committed, climbed with Him. Arriving at a quiet place, He sat down and taught His climbing companions. This is what He said:*

"You're blessed when you're at the end of your rope. With less of you there is more of God and His rule.

You're blessed when you feel you've lost what is most dear to you. Only then can you be embraced by the One most dear to you.

You're blessed when you're content with just who you are—no more, no less. That's the moment you find yourselves proud owners of everything that can't be bought.

You're blessed when you've worked up a good appetite for God. He's food and drink in the best meal you'll ever eat.

You're blessed when you care. At the moment of being 'careful,' you find yourselves cared for.

You're blessed when you get your inside world—your mind and heart—put right. Then you can see God in the outside world.

You're blessed when you can show people how to cooperate instead of compete or fight. That's when you discover who you really are, and your place in God's family.

You're blessed when your commitment to God provokes persecution. The persecution drives you even deeper into God's kingdom.

Not only that—count yourselves blessed every time people put you down or throw you

out or speak lies about you to discredit Me.
What it means is that the truth is too close
for comfort and they are uncomfortable. You
can be glad when that happens—give a cheer,
even!—for though they don't like it, I do! And
all heaven applauds. And know that you are
in good company. My prophets and witnesses
have always gotten into this kind of trouble"
(Matthew 5:1-12 MSG).

Attitude was the subject of training session number 1. He came with an attitude. He got it from His Father and checked it with his Father often. He didn't say anything His Father was not saying. Attitude would be everything. This family business of Kingdom enactment would necessitate an attitude reflecting His Father's attitude as well as His own. This business—Kingdom business—was the good news. This Gospel had an attitude. It was His Father's attitude, and He was present with that same attitude. Now those receiving His life must receive that same attitude.

1. Attitude Creates an Atmosphere

Our attitude is transmitted to everyone and everything around us. That is true in our families. It is true in the work place. It is true in church life. Attitude is like the thermostat that controls the atmosphere of a room.

2. Atmosphere Creates a Climate

As the atmosphere permeates everything in its sphere of influence, it creates a predictable climate. A climate is an experience of longer duration. Climates may last for months, as opposed to an atmosphere that may last only a short time.

3. Climate Creates a Culture

When a climate is sustained over a long period of time, a culture is created. Culture has more definitions and lasting qualities. As God's presence impacts regions or nations, the culture is engraved with His Word and His ways. Early America was so visited by God in the First Great Awakening that our founding fathers honored a part of that cultural value system.

Culture Welcomes Kingdom Expressions

Kingdom expressions accompany a culture of Christ's presence. A culture created out of the attitudes that Christ taught leads us to call for *"Your kingdom come. Your will be done on earth as it is in heaven"* (Matt. 6:10). Jesus did Kingdom deeds where welcome signs were posted. He didn't do those deeds where unbelief shut Him out. His disciples were trained to speak peace when they arrived at a new city. If peace was present, He was present. Without peace or His presence, they were to move to a new city (see Matt. 10:13-14). He always goes where He is welcome. Battering rams and bulldozers are not His way of entry.

Attitudes created between our ears create the gates and doors for His entrance. Once they are created, they are sustained, and as they are sustained, they are maintained. Maintenance is part of the cultural aspect of Kingdom life.

Kingdom consciousness starts inside us. *"The kingdom is inside you"* (Luke 17:21), Jesus told people who wanted a kingdom revolution that would overthrow Rome. Rome's foot was heavy on their necks. They wanted a change. But Jesus said they were looking for a temporary kingdom fix, whereas He was offering a Kingdom without end (see Dan. 4:3; John 18:36). When the Kingdom comes, what we think we need is not what we find we have. We find something better. It is not a change we need, but we need to be changed. We are changed into the same image from glory to glory (see 2 Cor. 3:18). But I will discuss this later.

STARTING WITH AN INTERNAL OPERATION

Kingdom life is not nearly as complicated as most people seem to want to describe it. Rather, childlikeness is the essence of Kingdom life.

> He called a little child and had him stand among them. And He said: "I tell you the truth, unless you change and become like little children, you will never enter the kingdom of heaven. Therefore, whoever humbles himself like this child is the greatest in the kingdom of heaven" (Matthew 18:2-4 NIV).

Understanding anything makes it seem simple. Complicated explanations usually come from incomplete understanding. My approach to this book is to keep it simple. The experiences I am relating came from simple approaches to events that are always "set-ups." Kingdom lives are the "set-ups" of God's provisions and plans. Everything I am relating seemed like God set it up; I simply entered into it.

Sophistication and complexity are not the characteristics Jesus modeled when He took a little child and stood him in the midst of them. If we take a good look at this child and then look at our kingdom complexities, we may discover why we see so little of His Kingdom and so much of our own.

The deep that calls unto the deep in Christ is still simple. If the Kingdom wasn't simple, it couldn't be managed by the childlike. There is, of course, a difference in the childish and the childlike. Being childlike is being spontaneous and filled with wonder. That comes out of seeing the marvel of a Kingdom bigger and better than we ever imagined because of the presence of Jesus being real to us within the operation.

There is no mind so brilliant that is not challenged by the brilliance of Christ's mind. Yet there is no mind so childlike that it cannot comprehend this gentle, loving person offering His mind once again.

A renowned thinker like Dr. Dallas Willard, head of the Philosophy Department of the University of Southern California, is challenged by the mind of Christ and His Kingdom. He wrote a classic treatise of Kingdom insights, *The Divine Conspiracy.*[2] Children and youth often operate with Kingdom attitudes and responses easier than sophisticated adults. Dallas Willard recognizes that children express from their hearts kingdom virtues: "The will, or heart, is the executive center of the self—also called freedom and creativity.

"Little children quickly learn to make things and to give them to those they love. If their souls are not crushed by life, as so many unfortuanately are, they will continue to do this throughout their lives."[3]

The Kingdom comes because Christ comes. He comes because we make Him welcome. He stays because a cultural climate is created to extend and express His Kingdom. Letting the mind be in us that was in Christ is letting His Kingdom come (see Phil. 2:5). His Kingdom includes transferring His attitude to us. We announce the news—the good news with an attitude.

Chapter 10

WHEN THE KINGDOM COMES—WHERE DOES IT GO?

Walking with Jesus through His life's engagements gives us a look at a Kingdom agenda.

The days of visitation at Graceland Baptist Church continued through the summer and into autumn. Waves of intensity accompany such visitations. As the intensity of His "announced presence" lessened, another wave would roll over the services or over the ministry teams that went out into the community doing deeds of kindness.

Practical things were done during the weeks of God's glory attending our gatherings. An economic downturn left a number of people without jobs and in need of funds for their basic requirements. Several times during those services, we took offerings to give assistance. Cars were repaired, new tires were purchased, rent and house payments were made, medical bills were paid, food was purchased, and hope was rekindled in people who were defeated.

A TIME OF TRANSITION

It became clear in the middle of September that it was time to discontinue the services on a weekly basis and allow Graceland to experience their usual schedule as a church. Elvis Marcum and his staff of people with such great qualities continued doing what was done in the services. People were ministered to at every level of their need. The counseling ministry was increased and extended to people throughout the area. Many with life-crippling bondages were freed. Families from across that region were transformed by the presence and power of the Lord. A church was shaken by His presence and Kingdom enactments. They modeled devotion to Him, His heart for all people, and a willingness to share with others their freedom and favor.

My own schedule extended to other places that invited me to come and share in their midst. Visitations of the Lord became frequent. At one point, five of these places with intensified awareness of His presence occurred at the same time. One of these places was Lake Country, where I pastored. Jesse McElreath, our associate pastor, had done a remarkable work in nurturing the Lord's expressions to us. It was his leadership and people's openness that resulted in sustained manifestations of His presence. Baptisms in the nearby Eagle Mountain Lake were frequent that summer, and many healings took place. Bill Miner, now 90 and in excellent health, instantly received complete restoration of his deaf ear on a Sunday morning.

Outpourings of the Lord also occurred in Plano, Texas; Dothan, Alabama; Mobile, Alabama; and Little Rock, Arkansas. I spent a lot of time on the phone with the leaders of those churches and flew or drove from place to place, speaking in extended services for a night or two. Those were days of advancement in what God wanted for His Church.

The "and suddenly" ushered in a major transition. A year or so later, the intensity of God's presence began to lift from Lake Country Baptist Church. Nor was that engaging presence expressed in the same measures in conferences where I spoke.

WHERE WAS JESUS ATTENDING CHURCH?

During that time, Jack Taylor, author, pastor, and long-time friend, was pastoring a start-up church in south Fort Worth. We met for fellowship and shared our personal journeys as well as the status of our churches. I asked him this question, "Is the Lord attending your church? I haven't found Him present in Lake Country in the way we have known in the past." He paused a moment and said, "No, I haven't noticed Him lately in our church, either." "Well, I wonder where He is attending?" I asked.

We decided to meet for prayer the next Saturday night and chose a lookout point over Fort Worth. During that prayer time, the Lord began speaking to me. With the glow of the city lying out before me, I heard the Lord say, "This is like a family farm that you know little about." With His use of language from my boyhood on the family farm, I heard in my spirit that I knew little about this family business. Family farms are owned jointly by all of the family. I never thought of what we did as work; it was just part of family life.

As a boy Jesus knew that He was called to the family business, the Father's business. Before me that night was a scene forever imbedded in my memory. Those many parts of a sprawling city, with the many zip codes that appeared on the addresses of thousands of families, were not owned by me. I didn't know the fields and conditions of my city. Our family farm required knowing each field. I wasn't engaged with the city. It was a place to live and a place to give leadership to a group of people in Lake Country. I knew my community, but not my city.

Before me was the realization that I was not doing my part. My Father's business was neglected because I knew so little about the city. My heart was overwhelmed by what I was hearing Him say. Tears washed my eyes as sorrow filled my heart. It is godly sorrow that leads to repentance (see 2 Cor. 7:10). I was experiencing a godly sorrow, and repentance came instantly. Repentance is always part of Kingdom recognition. We repent because the Kingdom is at hand. What we find in the Kingdom is far better than whatever we had or thought we had. It is a swap of something good or bad for something of greatest value. We sell all to purchase the pearl of greater value (see Matt. 12:46).

OWNING THE FAMILY BUSINESS

It was there that night that I took joint ownership of the family business in Fort Worth, Texas. I barely knew how to get from one field to the other, let alone the condition of each field on this family farm of city life. But in obedience to what the Lord had spoken, I stopped taking speaking engagements outside the church. And I went into the city to learn.

Soon I met a unique man named Gary Randle. He was a former basketball star at Texas Christian University and had the height to prove it at 6'9". With a heart reflecting God's heart, he served as a city policeman. His African American heritage and California roots gave him unique insight into the needs of the community of Fort Worth. With insights from his pastor, Dr. Tony Evans of Dallas, he was able to connect the dots of Kingdom issues to city problems. He drove me through the streets of Fort Worth, describing the condition of those "fields" on our Father's farm. He owned the farm as much as me and had owned it longer than me. Another world opened to my understanding.

Kingdom enlargement was occurring in my life without me knowing a term for it. Today, Gary Randle leads an inner-city ministry to black boys who have absentee fathers. An impressive campus exists in the "hood" that started in a deserted old crack house. The ministry is called Hope Farm. He has indeed brought much hope to "the farm" I saw that night overlooking the city. My life has been greatly shaped by this godly man whose keen mind and tender heart reflect so clearly the heart of God.

Through his contacts, I met men like Pastor Howard Caver of World Missionary Baptist Church, who has dared to develop a school in the heart of his neighborhood called Ecclesia Christian School. As a pastor and educator, he has a heart for the youth of his community as well as the elderly who need assisted living. So a nursing home center was begun by a

"Kingdom manager" who is willing for the Kingdom to come through him.

On the streets full of drug trafficking, at times I found myself at risk. Howard Caver and Ron O'Guinn, pastor in Bedford, Texas, told me I could not accompany them to certain meetings because of the racial tensions present in those days. Though I insisted on going with them, they flatly refused. It was a city filled with needs, divisions, and potential violence.

From the streets to the mayor's office, I learned of needs and issues facing the city of Fort Worth. Drug lords operated in neighborhoods where empty houses stood, indicating that no one would care what was "pushed" at that address. Many of those empty, dilapidated houses stood near World Missionary Baptist Church, where my dear friend, Howard, pastored. As he and I made our way through offices at Housing and Urban Development, we located assistance that was available. Habitat for Humanity came alongside us; the empty houses came down, and new houses changed the landscape. The drug lords moved out.

ONE PLACE JESUS WAS ATTENDING CHURCH

Weeks after my journey into the inner city began, I was invited to teach Bible to children in a government housing development. It was a hot July day. No air conditioning was available, and with sweat pouring off me in the midst of beautiful black children, I shared stories of Jesus doing His Father's business. It was there I discovered where Jesus was going to church. He was attending the places where needs were met in the people He valued and loved so completely. I heard Him say,

"What you do to the least of these, you have done it unto me"
(Matt. 25:40). These tiny children were the least. They were
not the adults I was accustomed to speaking to. Yes, there He
was, sitting with us in a Kingdom forum that required being
like a little child.

I had found the church Jesus was attending. But in that
process, I discovered that He hung out at the mayor's office,
too. Kay Granger, now congresswoman from Tarrant County,
made Him welcome. There were many offices at the regional
office of HUD where He was welcomed. From the Housing and
Urban Development office of Fort Worth, millions of dollars
were distributed into six surrounding states. With those dollars
came enormous potential to impact the Southwest. One of the
leaders then, Marcia Henohosa, gave invaluable assistance to
Howard Caver and me. She was a lady with a Kingdom heart
because Jesus ruled from within as her King.

PASTORING A CITY

It was not an easy transition to extend my role from a
church to a city. I sought the Lord's wisdom and guidance, and
He gave it graciously. The most difficult transition came in
church life. We had grown accustomed to the Lord visiting us,
and with His visitation, people came to bask in His presence.
Now He didn't come to us as regularly or as intently. We were
going to where He was hanging out. His location surprised us
at times.

One of the men of Fort Worth with a Kingdom heart was
Ernie Horn. He had a way of networking people, networking
ministries, relating to the government offices, and showing

love for the disenfranchised. Ernie became part of a Kingdom band of leaders in Fort Worth.

Churches were on the list for the Lord's engagements. If the Church is His Body, how can it be divided with amputations and quarantines? Out of that awareness, City Vision was formed as a coalition of churches from every ethnic, denominational, and socioeconomic expression. The coalition extended from Fort Worth and Arlington into southern Dallas.

We did services at times in the Water Gardens in the very heart of downtown Fort Worth where "street people" hung out. Ron O'Guinn gave a classic message there one day outlining how the Lord has a plan and purpose for every person living in the greater Metroplex of Dallas–Fort Worth. Later, Ron left the area to be director of reconciliation for Promise Keepers. He made a major contribution to racial reconciliation across the nation. Currently, he is back in Bedford, Texas, and is again leading a unique ministry in a church that is as expressive in the marketplace as in the gathering place. Sonset Noblesse Christian Ministries has a clear Kingdom vision.

Joint services for a number of substantial churches were held in the Will Rogers Auditorium, Fort Worth. Kay Granger had pledged, "Jim, if you ever need anything this office can supply, I will see you get it!" When I asked for the auditorium, she quickly supplied it. Churches like Restoration, with pastor Doug White, came all the way from Euless to be part of it. Churches meeting together on a Sunday morning made a statement with major volume. It said, "We are a united Body of Christ. We value other churches as much as our own. Every person in this region is important to God and to us. God has a plan for our city, neighborhoods, and families. We are gladly part of His plans!"

Doing joint services as we did on Sunday mornings means a church risks its offering for that Sunday. But people gave in their designated envelopes, and churches did receive the needed income to keep their budget balanced. An even greater risk is losing members and potential visitors who show up at their building, only to be greeted with a sign reading "Church services will be meeting at Will Rogers Auditorium." It was a gutsy call on the part of leaders who were part of the effort. We were pioneering a day when the Body of Christ is more about Kingdom connections than church divisions. Successful Church life was not as high a priority as Kingdom expressions.

As we fulfilled our servant roles across various areas, including assistance with housing, food distribution, establishment of furniture and clothing warehouses, and car repair and donation to people in need, another recognition occurred. It was apparent that our cities were offering services to the citizens through big-hearted police men and women, fire men and women, governmental officials, educators, and ministry leaders. We created a Life of Worth award and made presentations to selected people who had served us. Some of those citywide services were held on Sunday night at Birchman Avenue Baptist Church, where Miles Seaborn ably led the church. Sometimes parts of the Fort Worth Symphony assisted with music that took us to the outskirts of Heaven and brought some of Heaven to our gathering. Those celebration and recognition services of Kingdom exploits furthered the Kingdom enterprise. The Kingdom was coming.

THE KINGDOM GOES WHERE JESUS GOES

Where the Kingdom goes, when it comes, can't be predicted. The Kingdom's charted course was part of the discussion Jesus had with Nicodemus. He told him that only those who are born again can see the Kingdom (see John 3:3.). That occurrence was supernatural and of the Holy Spirit.

When asked further about the Spirit's birthing power, Jesus explained the similarity of the work of the Holy Spirit and the wind. The wind goes where it wants. It does announce its visitation with a sound, but not its destination. The wind goes where it chooses (see John 3:8). No one has devised methods of rerouting the wind. Better to ride the wind than try to control it. So it is with the choice of Kingdom destination. He who rules the Kingdom makes the choice. His choices are not made with our counsel, but with His sovereign wisdom.

Isaiah saw this as he looked forward as clearly as we can see it looking back. He may have seen more clearly than we do.

> *The grass withers, the flowers fade, but the Word of our God shall stand forever. O Crier of good news, shout to Jerusalem from the mountaintops! Shout louder—don't be afraid—tell the cities of Judah, "Your God is coming!" Yes, the Lord God is coming with mighty power; He will rule with awesome strength. See, His reward is with Him, to each as he has done. He will feed His flock like a shepherd; He will carry the lambs in His arms and gently lead the ewes with young. Who else has held*

the oceans in His hands and measured off the heavens with His ruler? Who else knows the weight of all the earth and weighs the mountains and the hills? Who can advise the Spirit of the Lord or be His teacher or give Him counsel? Has He ever needed anyone's advice? Did He need instruction as to what is right and best? (Isaiah 40:8-14 TLB)

Rather than being the Lord's advisors, we are much better off being the doers of His Word, which will stand whether we stand on it or not. His Word is not at issue; it will stand. The old saying, "We do not break the ten commandments, but are broken against them," is correct. God's Word is fixed, and it can fix us when we hear Him and obey Him. A thinker and seeker of truth once said, "It takes two to speak the truth—one to speak, and another to hear." If no one can speak the truth, no truth can be heard. If no one can hear the truth, no truth can live to liberate the hearer.

Where does the Lord go in Kingdom expressions? The answer is simply where He chooses. We are not asked to direct the Lord's visitation, but keep clear the path He chooses and make room for Him. Could it be we are wasting time trying to get Him to show up in places not of His choosing?

As I chose to walk out of the circles of conferences and "the moving of the Spirit in revival," I encountered varied reactions. Soon the people who wanted to attend another "feel-good" service with supernatural indicators that God was with us were saying, "Jim has lost the anointing." I had that discussion with a trusted friend. It was a spiritual check-up with one

I knew was qualified with God's wisdom, Word, and discernment. Was I really led by the Lord into the expanse of a city in need, or was I laying aside a mantle He had placed about me? I told my friend, "I did not fashion the mantle I wore; He did. I did not choose to lay it aside. I just wear it in a different setting with different results." My friend affirmed my conclusions.

OLD TIME RELIGION ISN'T GOOD ENOUGH

Jesus did not spend much time trying to change the religious order of His day. Most of His life was lived outside the walls of the capital city of religion, Jerusalem. He loved that city as He loved every city. With tears He wept over Jerusalem's unwillingness to gather under His protective cover as chicks would gather under the wings of a mother hen. Their refusal of His life and leadership rendered them vulnerable and in more danger than Sodom and Gomorrah (see Mark 6:11). They were expendable; His Kingdom was not.

Instead of hanging out in the religious places, He went to gala affairs such as a wedding. Water became wine when He added His presence to it (see John 2:7-11). Wine can just as easily become water when His presence is taken away. That is one issue we face today in the religious exercises of the Church. Wine, where He once was presenced, has been turned into water that is flat and lifeless.

Jesus went to the back side of society to find a man who lived in caves and was feared by all in the area. From that deranged man, He cast demons into swine feeding nearby. Swine were illegal by the laws of the country. Demons were illegal by the laws of the Kingdom. Jesus got rid of both (see Mark 5:2-15).

People were his objective. He was expanding the Kingdom so people could live within the benefits. His teaching made it very clear that people were where He placed His greatest value. Giving a cup of cold water was actually giving to Him. Visiting a person in prison, who probably was guilty of a crime, was visiting Him. Finding clothing for the naked was clothing Him (see Matt. 25:36). He was declaring Kingdom ordnances and benefits for the people He loved. Ministering to others equaled ministering to Him because of His identity with all people.

Mother Teresa caught the attention of the world by seeing Jesus in the people she lifted out of the streets of Calcutta, India. In a classic statement she declared, "Each one is Jesus in disguise:"[1] Jesus is indeed disguised in the needs of others waiting for our helping hand. Kingdom hands are extended to others rather than just gripping what we already have. We need to lose our grip on what we cling to. The Kingdom of God is full of provisions, but the key is holding them with a loose grip, ever ready to extend and release to others.

THE BIG PICTURE OF THE KINGDOM

There are no indicators in Jesus' teaching that only the supernatural can fit into the big picture of the Kingdom. Jesus was equally at home with the supernatural and with the practical. Much of the Church today that embraces the supernatural, which is a Kingdom characteristic, feels that the practical is a lesser enactment. They want the miraculous—things that can't be explained apart from God. God does not need unexplainable supernatural expressions to be God. He shows up all the time in the heavens above and on the earth we walk. Even nature has a natural display of His greatness (see Ps. 19:1-4). Supernatural displays are just as valid as the natural displays. Both are Kingdom operatives.

It is the balance of the natural and the supernatural that is the essence of Kingdom life. God is both powerful and practical. Kingdom life has both of these elements. Practical deeds may lead to supernatural power being manifested. Supernatural impartations from the Lord may lead to practical follow up. Both fit in the Kingdom agenda with a compatibility that God's wisdom and ways create.

A video documentary was given to me recently that stretched my thinking. The documentary, titled *Finger of God,* was produced by Darren Wilson, a guy who just wanted to know, "Does God still do the supernatural?" With honesty as a core value, and without professional experience, he began recording instances of Christ's supernatural power.[2]

One of the most gripping accounts I saw was of Rolland and Heidi Baker in their adopted country of Mozambique. Heidi Baker has remarkable gifting. I read one of her books and was impressed by her story. She grew up in California and could have been a model with her beauty and poise. Instead, with a heart for God, she obtained a PhD from King's College in London, England. She and Rolland then began serving among the poor and orphaned. Mozambique is actually the poorest nation of the world, and initially their primary focus was building orphanages for homeless children.[3]

An interview with a man who was raised from the dead opens the portion of this documentary that's filmed with the Baker's in Mozambique. His account was spoken in his language and translated into English. Three men attacked him and beat him to death. Hours after being pronounced dead, he was raised to life again. Though alive, a major problem existed. The beating was so bad that he had severe wounds and was very swollen. The prayer team led by the Bakers prayed again, and immediately the wounds were healed and the swelling left.

As I listened, my first thought was, *I have never seen a documentary of someone relating how they were raised from the dead.* Then Rolland Baker addresses the previous testimony with keen insight. He says, "Such an account of the dead being raised makes us feel uncomfortable, even feel a bit weird." He had assessed my thoughts as if he was there in person and not speaking from the video. Those thoughts may understandably be yours in the reading of this account. With careful thought about whether to use this as an illustration, I reflected on whether the "weird" would lose the reader. If C.S. Lewis, the gifted thinker and writer of *Miracles,* were here, I think he would say that the question is not so much whether a documentary can prove a miracle as much as whether our minds can accept the possibility of the supernatural.[4]

In the next portion of the film, the resurrected man relates that the police caught one of the men who had beaten him to death. Criminal justice in Mozambique called for him to be put to death, if his victim would act as a witness. Instead of revenge, the man once dead shared how he wanted the guilty man to be forgiven and freed. He went personally and told his attacker that he forgave him. Then he led him to know Christ personally. The once dead man was part of another expression of Christ's presence, an act of forgiveness extended to an undeserving man. I wonder even now, as I write, which is the greater miracle, the raising of the dead or the granting of forgiveness from the heart. One is the supernatural, the other is the practical application of part of the prayer, *"Forgive us our trespasses as we forgive those who trespass against us"* (Matt. 6:12).

That forgiving part of the prayer comes out of praying first, *"Thy will be done on earth as it is in heaven"* (Matt. 6:10). God's will enacted in Heaven calls for forgiveness, whatever the wrong may be. A man experiencing the life of Christ in him extended forgiveness because he saw the model of Heaven, which is the model of Kingdom life. The interaction of Heaven and earth is the essence of Kingdom reality. The Kingdom is coming from Heaven and going wherever Heaven decides it should go.

Chapter 11

THE SKYLINE OF
KINGDOM VISION

"Where heaven touches earth" is one of the meanings of the word *skyline*. Kingdom reality involves Heaven touching earth. Heaven touched earth when Jesus came to bring Heaven's order of life. His teaching in the model prayer indicates that God intends His will to be done on earth as it is in Heaven (see Matt. 6:19). This was the order and method by which Jesus lived His life. He saw what His Father was doing and did it with Him. He heard what His Father was saying and said it in agreement with Him (see John 5:19, 30, 36).

"Find out what God is doing and join Him," Henry Blackaby taught;[1] many embraced his ideal. Jesus modeled this principle. He did what was being done in Heaven. His delays in doing something, as in the case of raising Lazarus from the dead, came from the Father's instructions. Mary and Martha asked Him to come and heal their brother, Lazarus. Instead, He heard from His father that He was to demonstrate being *"the resurrection and the life"* (John 11:25). Healing was not the plan for Lazarus. Being raised from the dead was the plan (see John 11:14).

We seem to concentrate on what we think needs to be done and ask God to bless it. What God is not doing should be fairly obvious by now. Will God join our best efforts when we aren't on His page? Is He going to accommodate our plans when we are not even in the same chapter and, even worse, not even in the same book from which He is operating?

Can Heaven and earth be interactive? Are they supposed to be interfaced? Jesus thought so. He told Nathanael that he would see Heaven open and angels ascending and descending (see John 1:50-51). That conversation sprang from Jesus' vision of Nathanael under the fig tree and His insight into his pure heart. Nathanael was overwhelmed by Jesus' knowledge of him. Jesus could not only see him under a tree; He could also see him under a Heaven that opened up for exchanges. Kingdom operations are operations of Heaven's supplies and Heaven's guidance occurring on earth.

CAN GOD'S TEAM SEE HIM?

The writer of Hebrews pictured us in a great stadium with Heaven's residents cheering us on. *"We are surrounded by a great cloud of witnesses"* (Heb. 12:1) was the conclusion of the author, who was probably Paul. Life on this earth is a big stadium—a stadium with an open roof. The old Texas stadium, home of the Dallas Cowboys, was facetiously said to have an open roof so God could see His team play. No doubt God is watching us play. No doubt He owns the team. No doubt this is His franchise. His team is the Church, and His franchise is the Kingdom. When we have the right order of franchise goals, the right values, and the right authority, the team plays and wins.

More importantly than the fact that God can see His team, is the question, "Can His team see God?" The team's awareness of their ownership and His order for them leads to the Kingdom being at hand and on exhibit. Seeing Jesus creates Kingdom sight. Kingdom sight creates Kingdom guidance. Kingdom guidance creates Kingdom deeds.

As I prayed about how to treat and describe this subject, I was with a group of business men meeting for a noonday Bible study. It was a detailed study of the book of Galatians. The presence of the Lord grew so strong that the leader said, "We are on the edge of our seats." When the session ended, an astute man came to me with his carefully written notes. They were very accurate highlights of the teaching. Then he said, "I want you to see this last note I made!"

In a carefully scripted note I read, "Is this Heaven?"

So overwhelming was the presence of the Lord, he was asking, "Is this part of what Heaven is like?" My answer was, "Yes, this is part of the interaction of Heaven and earth that Jesus brings with His manifest presence." Of course Heaven will be greater and grander, and we will likely fall at His feet. John did on Patmos when he saw the glory of Jesus (see Rev. 1:17). But the point is, Heaven is open and interactive for us.

God's will on earth, as taken from the model of Heaven, was the model the early church knew and followed. A transformation came, and earth's practices were turned upside down (see Acts 17:6). If Heaven's way of doing things is not made clear, earth's way of doing things remains wrong side up.

AN OPEN DOOR TO HEAVEN

Our access to Heaven is gained in prayer. *"Our Father who is in Heaven"* (Matt. 6:9) is our beginning place. We call to God, recognizing the realm of Heaven and our Father God as the ruler. Kingdom life in Heaven is the model for Kingdom life on earth.

Prayer was such a part of Paul's life that he advocated we pray without ceasing (see 1 Thess. 5:17). Such a commitment to prayer was once very troubling to me. It seemed like an endless, gigantic task that I would never have a heart for or an ability to achieve. Actually, prayer is a track of consciousness that can play while we are multitasking. We can be having ongoing conversation with the Lord and doing other tasks, carrying on other conversations, driving in rush hour traffic, listening to others pray, watching the news, enjoying a ball game, or getting in a chosen isolated place of prayer.

Every Christian has access to Heaven. Taking advantage of that access is a choice we make. Prayer is a key to Kingdom operations, and it was modeled in the life of Jesus. Jesus did everything He did with excellence. He spoke as no one had ever spoken. He loved as no one had ever loved. He met needs as no one had ever met them. He changed social order by leading from the bottom up instead of from the top down. He healed people from every kind of disease. He freed people from demonic bondage. He showcased life as God in human flesh and man as normal.

Of all the things that He ever did with excellence—only one thing caused the disciples to ask Him to teach them how to do it, too. They wanted to know how to pray like He prayed (see Luke 11:1).

And it is this part of His life on earth that He continues to do at the right hand of the Father, now in Heaven. He continues to pray. He prayed as He lived on earth, calling Heaven's supplies into earth's needs. Now He lives to pray from Heaven, calling for supplies at His command to reach earth's needs.

> *Therefore He is able also to save to the uttermost (completely, perfectly, finally, and for all time and eternity) those who come to God through Him, since He is always living to make petition to God and intercede with Him and intervene for them* (Hebrews 7:25 AMP).

It is overwhelming for me to realize that Jesus ordered Kingdom operations on this earth through prayer. He continues to do so in Heaven. Now His orders for operations come from the supply room. On earth He was calling out from the need's room for Heaven's supplies. Our God shall supply our every need out of His riches in glory in Christ Jesus (see Phil. 4:19). Need is connected to His supply.

PRAYER IS A WIRELESS
CONNECTION TO GOD

The ability to intercede for others is the highest order of service we can offer. Jesus modeled that service as He modeled other remarkable ministries. Intercession is taking a position between God and others and connecting them. We connect to God in prayer, and from that connection, we can connect others as well.

Intercession is illustrated in Joseph's life very clearly. Kingdom operations were also modeled. When stripped of his many colored coat and sold into slavery by his jealous brothers, he remained connected to God. Though disconnected from everything familiar and important to him, he remained connected to God. His faith in God was the vital connection.

Miles separated him from his family and countrymen. Walls of cultural differences separated him from his own people. Massive idols to gods of every kind towered above him. But none of the hindrances could keep him from the presence of God. Distance did not separate him. Culture did not redefine him. Idols did not appeal to his faith. Out of his steadfast connection to God, he remained connected in his heart to his family and to his people.

Because of that connection to God, Joseph rose through the ranks to rule Egypt under the Pharaoh as prime minister. With power and wealth in his hands, he stretched those hands out to his brothers in forgiveness and restoration. To his countrymen he offered food and favor for survival. His connection to the resources of Egypt allowed him to connect a people he loved to the same resources.

Not only did he save the Pharaoh and the people of Egypt, but he saved the nation of Israel and brought them into the blessings his wisdom had amassed. He had interceded by joining God in prayer. In his intercession, he paved the way for his nation to be preserved (see Acts 7:9-14). There is not a scripture for my statement. It is an interpretation based on facts.

No wonder Jesus lives to intercede. Out of the greatest victory ever won and the greatest bounty ever amassed, Jesus lives to connect us to the rights and riches of His Kingdom. We are made joint heirs of all His accomplishments and all His riches. What belongs to Him belongs to us. Thus, we have not because we ask not (see James 4:2). It is not the lack of anything that keeps us from having what we need. It is only the lack of asking and receiving.

THE ART OF ASKING

When we pray, we always find Jesus already there and praying when we arrive. Our joining Him gets us where the action is. We are not praying to God; we are praying with God.

Usually, we only think of praying to God. But Jude shows us in his epistle that we are joining God and praying with Him.

> *But you, dear friends, build yourselves up in your most holy faith and **pray in the Holy Spirit**. Keep yourselves in God's love as you wait for the mercy of our Lord Jesus Christ to bring you to eternal life* (Jude 20-21 NIV).

When we pray in the Holy Spirit, we are being guided in prayer by the Lord through the Holy Spirit. Praying in the Holy Spirit is praying with God's guidance and God's thoughts offered to us. How to pray and what to pray for are given to us by Him.

These same insights are found in other Scriptures as well. Paul wrote:

> *And **pray in the Spirit** on all occasions with all kinds of prayers and requests. With this in mind, be alert and always keep on praying for all the saints* (Ephesians 6:18 NIV).

This guidance in prayer is for "all times" or "all occasions," not just for some extraordinary enablement from the Lord.

In Romans we are reminded why this kind of praying is so important.

> *In the same way, the Spirit helps us in our weakness. We do not know what we ought to pray for, but the Spirit Himself intercedes for us with groans that words cannot express. And He who searches our hearts knows the mind of the Spirit, because the Spirit intercedes for the saints in accordance with God's will* (Romans 8:26-27 NIV).

The Holy Spirit has never missed praying the will of God. He always knows what God is doing and wants done on earth.

FAITH CONNECTS HEAVEN AND EARTH

Without faith it is impossible to please God (see Heb. 11:6). Whatever is not of faith is sin (see Rom. 14:23). There are two sins in faithlessness toward God. Without faith in God, we are putting faith in our own self efforts. Clinging to our righteousness is a refusal to receive God's righteousness as a gift in Christ.

The second violation is that we have faith, but it is directed to another source. No faith in God means we have faith offered to someone or something else. That resting place of faith is sin because a rival of God is created. Idolatry has occurred. That is why John ends his epistle in First John 5:21 with this final thought, *"Dear Children, keep yourselves from idols"* (NIV).

Jesus declared that at the root of sin is a choice to not believe God. He said the Holy Spirit would come and show us sin, righteousness, and judgment (see John 16:8). He then defined sin, *"Sin because they do not believe in Me"* (John 16:9).

Not believing God means we believe something. It may be our own reasoning and conclusions. It may mean we believe our own hurting hearts more than we believe God's comforting love. It may mean we believe our sickness is greater than His power to heal. It may mean we want our guilt more than His forgiveness.

Jesus came looking for faith on earth. The greatest faith He found was in a least likely person. When a Roman centurion asked Him to heal his servant, Jesus started to go to his house to heal the servant. This official of Rome said, "No I am not worthy of your visit to my house. You don't need to be present, just send your word and he will be healed." The servant was immediately healed (see Matt. 8:5-13).

Two times Jesus marveled in His life. He marveled at this man's faith, and He marveled at other people's unbelief. *"I have not found such great faith, not even in Israel,"* Jesus said (Matt. 8:10). He was looking for faith, and He found the greatest amount of it in a man without religion.

Religion does not create faith. In fact, religion usually eliminates faith because it creates an alternate system of hope. Religion is the greatest enemy to the Kingdom. It is a system of belief and discipline that often appeals to the best in a person. But that order of religious effort is the enemy of God. As I said previously, Christian religion is no different than any religion. I am not talking about a relationship with Jesus, but a system of rules and beliefs based on performance. It is a system that does not have Christ at the center and, thus, does not manifest the Kingdom actualized.

Paul describes that tragic turning from God to idols in Romans 1:21-25. It can take place within the frame work of the best efforts in church life. One of America's most gifted communicators, Craig Groeschel, pastor of Life Church.TV, in Edmond, Oklahoma, has acknowledged that he became a practical atheist.[2] He was doing what he did out of his own skills and gifts without God. His heart of honesty and humility ought to cause all of us to hit the pause button and ask if we are only doing things for God or if we are experiencing God doing things for us.

It is not our works God wants. God wants to make us His workmanship so He can do His work through us. We are created in Jesus Christ unto good works (see Eph. 2:10).

These good works are His works from within us. His works are done because of faith. Faith connects us to His provisions and power. Kingdom life is Jesus in action. His action comes from our faith resting in His ability. At the heart of Kingdom activity is faith confidently resting in the authority of Jesus Christ. He is the author and finisher of our faith, and He is the receiver of our faith.

FAITH IS THE FOUNDATION FOR THINGS HOPED FOR

Faith is the substance of things hoped for and the evidence of things not seen (see Heb. 11:1). Faith never goes anywhere without a companion called hope. They never go anywhere without another companion called love. Faith, hope, and love are eternal because all are of God from God and display God.

Hope is a significant part of the Kingdom operation. Other kingdoms may promise hope, but cannot supply it. God's Kingdom fills sails with the winds of hope. Hope is a necessary part of faith. When there seems to be no hope, we can choose to believe God. Abraham did that. It was a choice. Romans 4:18 gives the account. Three different translations use different words, but reach the same conclusion: *"Against all hope, Abraham in hope believed..."* (NIV); *"[For Abraham, human reason for] hope being gone, hoped in faith..."* (AMP); *"Who against hope believed in hope..."* (KJV).

Robert Frost said, "Two roads diverged in a wood, and I—/ I took the one less traveled by, / and that has made all the difference."[3] Abraham stood at that fork in the road. One road read "No Hope"; the other road read "Hope." He took the road less traveled by, the road of hope. It made all the difference for him, just as the poet reported.

We are at a fork in the road in America. Economic decisions have created a shakedown. Safety from terrorism no longer exists. Cultural choices have left our days of safe neighborhoods gone forever. Our fork in the road can lead us anew to God. As we stand and peer into the future, one sign reads, "No hope." But then with eyes of faith we see another sign come into focus, "Hope." This is a sign posted by the Lord and given to His people. Details on the sign reads, *"Seek first the kingdom of God and His righteousness and all these things shall be added to you"* (Matt. 6:33).

The difference in hope and no hope is the seeking factor. What we ask for is what we get. What we seek for is what we find. What we knock on is what opens to us (see Matt. 7:7-8). Seeking carries the word *see* in it. Seeking leads to *seeing*. I have a much harder time finding things in grocery stores or even around the house than Jane does. She finds so much more than I do because she seeks with a *seeing* of details that I miss. She also seems to have a schematic layout of most stores, as if she is a co-owner. We too have access to the schematic of Kingdom layouts as co-owners, if we claim them.

Seeking first the Kingdom is a *seeing* issue. When we seek, we are asking to see. When we see, we have found. Seeking is over when sight comes. It is the difference for hunters and fishers as well. For most people, they have little to say about their latest "finding trip" or their latest "catching trip." So much more time is spent hunting and fishing than finding and catching that the only word we know to use connotes a search.

Finding is our need. Catching is our need in the Body of Christ right now. What are we hunting for? What are we seeking to catch? All of the materials I read that have been written in the past tell us to hunt for revival.

WHY THERE IS HOPE AND HOW TO HOPE

A clear cycle of having hope and taking that hope to the finish line is found in Romans chapter 5. It is not insignificant that all breakthroughs in past works of God have come out of the distilled revelation of Romans. Like Siamese twins, Romans and "revivals" have been born together. They are attached at the heart and attached at the hip. Sometimes people are reading Romans and get their invitation to enter a new dimension of awareness of the Lord. Others enter that dimension of an awareness of the majesty of God's personhood and are led to study Romans for clarification. I was studying Romans in West Plains, Missouri, with great concern about how I could treat chapters 6 and 7 when the Lord visited us as described in the opening of this book. My concern was replaced with His Presence, and chapter 6 became experiential, not theological. Parts of chapter 7 I did not understood for years, but I left what I didn't understand to His understanding, believing He would share when the timing was right.

Operative faith leads to hope, and Paul embraced that in his heart and put the pencil to the parchment to declare it.

Therefore, since we have been justified through faith, we have peace with God through our Lord Jesus Christ, through whom we have gained access by faith into this grace in which we now stand. And we rejoice in the hope of the glory of God. Not only so, but we also rejoice in our sufferings, because we know that suffering produces perseverance; perseverance, character; and character, hope. And hope does not disappoint us, because God has poured out His love into our hearts by the Holy Spirit, whom He has given us (Romans 5:1-5 NIV).

Cycles of God's leading often leave us feeling like we are going in circles. We feel that way because we are. God does not lead on a continuum of getting from one point to the other in the shortest possible time and distance. He can take all the time He wants and all of the territory He possesses. So here is a cycle of the Christian life charted for us to see. It is like the face of clock. At the 12 o'clock position we have hope. Our hope is for the glory of God. In the glory of God is the presence of God visiting us.

We move to the 3 o'clock position and there we experience pressure. It is the word *thlipsis* in the original language. It is the picture of the pressure created by the wine press or the olive press. Both are designed to get a desired quality from the grape or the olive.[4] Pressure allows a desired quality or presence to be released from us, the presence of the Lord.

At 6 o'clock on this cycle, we arrive at a place of perseverance. It is time in the journey to keep going, regardless of how tough the place we are in may seem. Perseverance is our going on with God. We have reason to press on with God because He is ever caring for us.

Nine o'clock follows. Here we have proven character. Character is an essential quality for those who bear the family name and wield the family authority. God wants His kids to be kids with His character, proven in the tests of life. From 9 o'clock we return to 12 again. This time around, we not only have hope, but we have a bigger hope. We have seen the Lord use us to kill a lion and a bear. Now we are ready with a greater faith and an enlargement of hope to kill a giant, as David did. Hope for His glory is the ultimate anticipation of things being different.

I will deal with the glory factor of Kingdom qualities in the next chapter. God's glory is our greatest hope.

LOVE CONDITIONS A KINGDOM ATMOSPHERE

The Kingdom operation requires a right attitude, as I have already described. That attitude is primarily love. It is the central element of a Kingdom atmosphere because it is the essence of God's being.

God does not choose to love. He *is* love. For Him to decide whether to love or not would be like deciding whether to be God or not. He is already God. That is settled. Since He is love, He doesn't need to choose what He already is. God is love. His Kingdom is a Kingdom reflecting His greatest attribute. The greatest of these inseparable friends (faith, hope, and love) is love. God is love, and love reflects God's greatness.

God's love is shed abroad in the heart by the Holy Spirit who is given to us (see Rom. 5:5). Love is the greatest need of our human experience. Thus it is equally the greatest gift we can give. When the presence of Christ permeates any setting, there is always the visitation of His love.

Even if He is correcting or disciplining us, He is still loving us. Whom the Lord loves, He disciplines or trains (see Heb. 12:6-8). The attractiveness of the early church is not what we are known for today. How they loved one another was the brand of their distinctiveness. That distinctiveness was magnetic. It drew people to know the Lord, who was the source of their love. As new creations in Christ, we have the original make-up of God's creation immediately in our spirits. It is this deposit of God's presence in us that draws others to life as God intended it originally.

The late Dr. Adrian Rogers had a great way of describing the creative miracle of God in making new creations. He shared how the new birth reverses the fall of Adam and Eve. The deliberate decision of Adam resulted in them dying immediately in their spirits, progressively in their souls, and eventually in their bodies. With the chuckle Adrian often used that let you know he was enjoying the truth as much as you, I have heard him say in conferences: "We are made alive immediately in our spirits, progressively in our souls, and eventually in our bodies."

Indeed the God-shaped blank in our lives is filled immediately in our spirits. We are new creations, and the God of the universe is indwelling us. Our souls are saved progressively as we learn to allow the Spirit to rule. Our bodies are not immortal, but eventually that same quickening power will give us bodies like Jesus. It will be a body of flesh and bones with the life cycle of the Holy Spirit instead of blood. In the meantime, healing is part of the benefits of health assurance for our mortal bodies. The best part of the assurance plan is that we get immortal bodies when the originals are ready for replacement.

New creations have God's DNA restored to them. It is His DNA or genetic chain that contains His love. His life in us brings love to us experientially. Charles G. Finney described it as liquid love being poured over him.[5] Love is no longer merely a word or a concept, but love becomes an experience that impacts our emotions as well as our minds. God is loving us; we are loving God. This is the atmosphere created in Kingdom awareness.

God is love. Our life in Him begets love's triangle. We love God because He first loved us (see 1 John 4:19). We love ourselves no longer from selfishness, but in honor of His love for us. We love others because we have enough love to extend it to our neighbors. In fact, we have enough love to love our enemies.

Karl Barth summarizes God's love nature:

> Love for the neighbor is love for him in all his strange, irritating, distinct createdness... Love is eternal leveling righteousness, because it justifies no man according to his desire. Love edifies the fellowship because it seeks fellowship only. Love expects nothing, because it has already reached the goal. Love does not intend, because it has already done. Love asks no questions, it already knows. Love does not fight, it is already victor. Love is not Eros, that lusteth ever, it is Agape that never faileth.[6]

When we run low on love, we load up again by letting Christ release His love from within. Nothing can separate us from the love of God, that is, nothing outside of ourselves (see Jude 21). The valve of His love can be shut off within us. Love reaches us, but we won't let His love in or out.

We have done a far better job telling people how to let Jesus in than we have in telling them how to let Jesus out. Letting Jesus out is letting the life and love He shares with us be shared again with others. The Kingdom coming creates a love-based behavior for all we do. This love-based motivation becomes the order for Church life born out of the Kingdom overlay of purpose. Reaching out to people is based on what God can do for them, not what they can do for us.

Paul was so overwhelmed by the love of God for his own people, he was willing to be accursed or go to hell instead of them (see Rom. 9:1-3). That is evangelism based on God's love. Evangelism based on reaching a quota for statistical standards is a self-serving form of religion. A full dose of God's love is greatly needed to break the chains of tradition that bind us.

A church that has grown to 200,000 people and is rich with a heritage of reaching people with the love of Christ was the setting where I recently heard my pastor, Bob Roberts of Northwood Church, Keller, Texas, describe his journey across barriers of prejudice and fear to love people. We were in Abidjan, Ivory Coast, Africa with Pastor Dion Robert and the Protestant Baptist Church. Bob Roberts was a featured speaker. He shared how once he knew a prejudice toward the communist people of Vietnam. That prejudice was replaced by the love of Christ, which led him to make Vietnam his second country. Then he described an ever-more unlikely extension of love reaching out from his heart to others. His message of learning to love Muslims along with all people groups led to a standing ovation from about 2,000 pastors.

His words that evening are partly highlighted in his most recent book, *Real Time Connections*. "Through my experiences in Vietnam, I had come to love 'communist atheists' and learned not to fear them, but Muslims—well that's another story."

Through a chain of events he was asked to assist with humanitarian efforts in Afghanistan. Reluctantly, he agreed to go:

> Despite my initial fears, within a short time I fell in love with the Afghani people. Their radically different culture intrigued me—the food, the smells, the landscape, the clothing, the sound of the language. At one point during my trip I was in the Afghan desert with a group of imams—They began asking me about my religious beliefs. In the midst of our discussion, we came to the time for prayer, and the imams began spreading out their rugs on the desert floor to pray. Since it was prayer time, I followed suit and took to my knees praying to Jesus while they said their prayers. In many ways, this was a turning point for me.

I have found that real love motivates us to seek understanding. When you truly care about someone, you do whatever you can to understand them. And for the first time in my life I was actively trying to love Muslims. And as I sought to love them, I began seeing supposedly fearsome Muslims in a different light, the light of God's kingdom. I saw them not as fearsome angry people, but as people whom God loves and wants to reconcile to himself.[7]

That love for Muslims has led to doors opening for Bob Roberts to sit with world leaders of the Muslim, Jewish, and Christian faith to discuss ways to end violence and bring cooperative solutions to long standing tensions in the Middle East.

Perfect love casts out all fear (see 1 John 4:18). The opposite of love is not hate, but fear. Hate is an emotion created by fear or a demonic presence that may use both fear and hate. Our emotion of hate is a way of saying, "I will protect myself from what I fear with hate. Hate will not let me get hurt by those I fear." That premise is wrong. Hate creates more hate because it generates more fear. Hate will neither protect us nor hurt those we hate. It is like drinking poison to cure a stomach ache.

Fear-filled lives cannot be managers of God's Kingdom business. Love-filled lives are show-cases of grace, mercy, and peace. God's grace is extended, God's mercy is given anew each morning, and God's peace quiets every storm. The Kingdom coming is not eating from the old menu of meat and drink, but trying a new menu of righteousness, peace, and joy (see Rom. 14:17). The cook is the Holy Spirit. Taste and see that the Lord is good (see Ps. 34:8).

Chapter 12

LIGHT TO SEE
THE KINGDOM

The glory of God is the light to see God's Kingdom. God's glory and God's Kingdom are interactive because both are manifestations of His presence. His presence in glory brings the light with which we see His Kingdom.

Without God coming personally to illuminate the operative Kingdom, we would miss it altogether. God has never stopped saying, "Let there be light." Without Him furnishing the light, we haven't the clarity to see what exists. God is not creating the Kingdom. It is already created. It is a remarkable panorama to watch the Kingdom of God from eternity past enter into time as we know it, unfold in various types and shadows, and then appear again in Christ's activities. As the curtains of Revelation open and eternity future appears, we see an eternal Kingdom clearly operative. The interactive engagements of Heaven and earth are interactions of both time and eternity.

His Kingdom is within us. His glory is within us. His Kingdom is resident because Christ is resident. His glory is resident because Christ is resident. Christ in you is the hope of glory (see Col. 1:27).

Kingdom reality is an inside job. Consciousness of Christ's life and Kingdom enactment starts inside us. Whatever we call the reality that occurs, the reality begins with the presence of Christ letting His light shine within us. That light makes us the light of the world as well.

LOOKING FOR CHRIST IN THE WRONG DIRECTION

Most of the focus on Christ is either the Christ of the past or the Christ of the future. Many, with a nostalgia that enhances Israel's tourist industry, go back to take the steps where He once walked. I too have enjoyed the tour and have led others on the tour. But we have the same need as those who went to the tomb early in the morning. They looked in the wrong place. Thinking He was where they last saw Him, they went to the tomb. They looked in the wrong tense. He was the Christ of the past. Going back to the past for one more look will not let us see Him. We need to hear the angel for ourselves, *"He is not here, He is risen"* (Luke 24:6).

Or we look wistfully to the throne where He sits in reigning residency. We live with the anticipation that He is going to get up off the throne and begin making His way back to earth.

Many are checking His travel schedule constantly. Attempts are made to read the signs of His coming. Israel is usually the focus of His return. Many believe He will base His booking to return on what is happening with Israel and their neighbors.

The Last Days Are Here Again was the tongue-in-cheek title for a book written as people made all kinds of predictions based on Y2K.[1] The "last days" have lasted much longer than anyone ever projected and are not likely to end anytime soon. It is time to get over the "last days" and to get up to speed with "these days." These days are days for His life from within to have expression. There is the hope of glory.

Neither the backward look nor the forward look will locate Him. The hope of glory is not the historic timeframe of Him walking on earth in a body like ours. It is the fact He is here now in us. He is the Christ in you giving you the hope of glory (see Col. 1:27).

WHAT DO WE CALL THE SIGHTINGS OF JESUS?

Seeing Him has been called *revival* for decades. Revivalists have shared the stories of His appearing and claimed that He wants to do it again. I have been one of them. *Awakening* is another term we have used to describe this newly-found clarity of vision.

Neither of those terms is wrong. There is a reviving of that which has lost vigor and vitality. Awakenings have occurred and with them new vision. Any sighting of Christ has untold benefits. Calling it revival or awakening does not alter His visitation with accompanying manifestations. But the problem is that the terms are inadequate to describe the big picture of what God wants to do. Is the Kingdom by any other name still the Kingdom? Is a rose by another name still a rose? I think so. Yet, if I want a rose, yet ask for a daffodil, how can my order be filled?

Has "the Kingdom coming" been called revival or awakening? Why would I even bother to raise the issue? I raise it because I think we have labored with concepts and the anticipation of something that is not as great as God has in mind. Not only that, but I also believe we do not have a biblical foundation to support what we have called revival. Revival, as we know it or think of it, is designed to rescue the Church at worst and salvage the sagging statistics of the Church at best. I do not need to build a case for the needs of the Church. From mega-churches to mini-churches, we face major issues. While mega-churches reach gigantic size, overall church attendance is on the decline. Communities and cities in the shadow of the largest churches may go untouched and unchanged.

PRAYER EDITING

Prayer editing is required because of our prayer handicap. We do not know what to pray for. From groanings that are unutterable or from oratorical declarations that could be printed in the anthology of beautiful prayers, the Holy Spirit must edit our praying. I think the Holy Spirit is saying to the Father, "They are asking for revival and awakening. What they really want is for the Kingdom to come." The Holy Spirit speaks up for us because we don't know how to ask or what to ask for. Even when we ask for the wrong thing, the Lord gives us what we need.

The cripple at the Beautiful Gate was asking for money in his cup. That was what he thought he needed. Peter and John didn't have what he wanted, but what he needed. He wanted alms. He needed legs. They said, *"What we have we give to you"* (Acts 3:6). What they had was the transferred authority of Jesus to supply legs. We ask for what we think we need, and the Lord graciously gives us what we really need.

RECEIVING A KINGDOM IS BETTER

I have come to the conclusion that receiving a Kingdom is far better than praying down revival. Here is what God said about this receiving principal:

> *Therefore, since we are receiving a kingdom that cannot be shaken, let us be thankful, and so worship God acceptably with reverence and awe* (Hebrews 12:28 NIV).

Praying down Heaven-sent revival has long been a formula for spiritual breakthrough. How long the formula has been used is an interesting study. It is not a formula that goes back to Paul and the early church. After comparing this formula to Paul's understanding, I have concluded that we have added to the script and convinced ourselves that Paul was an advocate of revival. First of all, Paul was not a revivalist. He was birthing churches, not reviving them. Kingdom acceleration was his goal, not revival. Foundations already laid were not his calling. He engaged in foundation repair, but his first choice was to lay a new foundation.

Second, he was calling for the appropriation of the rights that belong to a child of God. He saw the finished work of Christ as belonging to every child of God. There was no first class, business class, and coach class on the Christian Airlines he rode. Each one in Christ had the same seating as every other person in Christ.

Third, when a church's actions were a contradiction to their being in Christ, he did not urge them to pray down revival. Corinth was a church that was bringing shame rather than fame to Christ. If revival could have changed the church, the Holy Spirit would surely have led Paul to suggest that they needed a revival. He could have offered to come and speak or send one of his team to them.

The manifest presence of Christ brought Paul to place his faith in Him. In the light of that presence, he received Christ within his life. Out of that relationship and the revelation of knowing Christ came the reality of who Christ was in him and who he was in Christ.

The prescription he wrote for the sick church at Corinth is significant. As a church doctor he had a revealing diagnosis. They were not acting like who they were. So, he told them who they were.

> *To the church of God which is at Corinth, to those who are sanctified in Christ Jesus, called to be saints, with all who in every place call on the name of Jesus Christ our Lord, both theirs and ours: Grace to you and peace from God our Father and the Lord Jesus Christ* (1 Corinthians 1:2-3).

They were set aside and sanctified, and even though they were not acting like it, they were saints like the saints everywhere. This was not the second-class-saints church.

He also acknowledged his thanksgiving to God for them:

> *I always thank God for you because of His grace given you in Christ Jesus. For in Him you have been enriched in every way—in all your speaking and in all your knowledge—because our testimony about Christ was confirmed in you. Therefore you do not lack any spiritual gift as you eagerly wait for our Lord Jesus Christ to be revealed. He will keep you strong to the end, so that you will be blameless on the day of our Lord Jesus Christ. God, who has called you into fellowship with His Son Jesus Christ our Lord, is faithful* (1 Corinthians 1:4-9 NIV).

Thanksgiving to God was uppermost in his mind. He was not praying against them, but praying for them, and that started with thanksgiving. Many qualities of the Corinthian church did warrant thanksgiving to God. They were accessing God's provisions. They didn't need a thing that they didn't already have. God was faithful to them and was not about to abandon them.

But another issue flowed from Paul's pen. Soon he described their misconduct. Who they were was forgotten, and they acted as carnal people who did not have the life of Christ in them at all. They were a church contradicting their birthright.

Was Paul setting them up for a trip to the "woodshed of discipline"? No. Rather, his commendation and gratefulness to God were based on this:

> *But it is from Him that you have your life in Christ Jesus, Whom God made our Wisdom from God, [revealed to us a knowledge of the divine plan of salvation previously hidden, manifesting itself as] our Righteousness [thus making us upright and putting us in right standing with God], and our Consecration [making us pure and holy], and our Redemption [providing our ransom from eternal penalty for sin]. So then, as it is written, "Let him who boasts and proudly rejoices and glories, boast and proudly rejoice and glory in the Lord"* (1 Corinthians 1:30-31 AMP).

They were in Christ, and they had nothing to boast or glory in except Him. He was enough for them, just as He was enough for saints at Ephesus or Thessalonica. God made Christ wisdom for us, righteousness for us, and consecration for us. We don't appear outside of Him to God.

We never lose our position of being in Christ, but God holds us responsible for our actions and lets us know the issue. Guilt is not the guide to a life of victory, but grace. Grace shows us how we contradict the reality of who we are when we sin. That is why this corrective letter was written. Paul was saying, "Here is who you are! Act like it!"

They got it! They did start acting like who they were. His reminder of who they were led him to commend them in Second Corinthians. Light had come and they could see (see 2 Cor. 3:2-6).

SITTING DOWN TO
RECEIVE THE KINGDOM

Another of Paul's major letters was written to Ephesus. It reveals the victory Christ won and shares with every Christian. Ephesians depicts the interchange between Heaven and earth more clearly than any other book in Scripture.

Paul described to the Ephesians his own birthright in Christ. Paul knew who he was, where he lived, and how to behave. He was seated in Christ in the heavenlies, and he was strong in the Lord (see Eph. 3:6-6:10).

Paul knew the interchangeable relationship between Heaven and earth. He had a physical address in Rome. But he lived in the heavenlies, in the spiritual realm of Christ's enthronement. You could not visit Paul in Rome. He didn't live there. If you wanted to find him at home, you had to visit him in the heavenlies. Paul's experience illustrates the interaction of Heaven and earth. He lived in the heavenlies and on earth at the same time.

This is the central truth of Ephesians. Christ has ascended to a reigning position and reserved us seats to sit with Him. We are raised up to sit with Him. This is a pivotal truth of the Christian life and a pivotal truth to the realization of Kingdom authority. Where Christ sits, we sit.

And He raised us up together with Him and made us sit down together [giving us joint seating with Him] in the heavenly sphere [by virtue of our being] in Christ Jesus (the Messiah, the Anointed One). He did this that He might clearly demonstrate through the ages to come the immeasurable (limitless, surpassing) riches of His free grace (His unmerited favor) in [His] kindness and goodness of heart toward us in Christ Jesus (Ephesians 2:6-7 AMP).

Paul saw us seated to reign. So he was not on a quest for revival at Ephesus, but on a quest for them to experience what he knew. His prayer life was born out of the revelation he had received. What he prayed for this church is what needs to be prayed for every church. Great significance should be attached to this prayer. It is a prayer for us today as much as it was for them then; that is why it is recorded for our eyes as well.

I have not stopped giving thanks for you, remembering you in my prayers. I keep asking that the God of our Lord Jesus Christ, the glorious Father, may give you the Spirit of wisdom and revelation, so that you may know Him better. I pray also that the eyes of your heart may be enlightened in order that you may know the hope to which He has called you, the riches of His glorious inheritance in the saints, and His incomparably great power for us who believe. That power is like the working of His mighty strength, which He exerted in Christ when He raised Him from the dead and seated Him at His right hand in the heavenly realms, far above all rule and authority, power and dominion, and every title that can be given, not only in the present age but also in the one to come. And God placed all things under His feet and appointed Him to be head over everything for the church, which is His body, the fullness of Him who fills everything in every way (Ephesians 1:16-23 NIV).

Because this is a prayer for you and me today, I am going to highlight it in the present tense:

- He prays for wisdom and revelation for us to know Christ better.

- He prays that the eyes of our hearts will be open to the hope of Christ's calling.

- He prays that we may see that we are the glorious inheritance given to God through Christ. We are what God most wanted and obtained as an inheritance through Christ's purchase of us.

- He prays for us to know the great power available to those who believe. This is the power that was demonstrated when Jesus was raised from the dead.

- He prays for us to see Christ raised and seated in triumph.

- He prays that we will see everything under the feet of Christ and the Church. As the Church, we are His Body, sitting with everything under our feet as well.

Praying for revival would have been asking for too small a venue. Paul was seeing a Kingdom-proportioned victory that every Christian would share in through their reigning rights. Paul was praying a Kingdom-sized prayer.

Unlimited seating still remains. Our need is for eyes to see and hearts to believe that what is ours comes through receiving.

WHAT DO WE NEED?

Our need is for the Kingdom to come. The reason the Kingdom coming is greater than revival is that revivals never last. The Kingdom is unshakeable and never-ending. All great "revivals" come and go. The exception of that may be China, where the Church went underground and did not take on the structural limitations of the institutional church; thus, it still proliferates today. That means it became more Kingdom-centered than church-centered. Even national revivals, such as in South Korea, only last for a limited time.

The "revival" of Argentina that swept thousands upon thousands into the family of God lasted for seven or eight years. I visited one of the churches in Buenos Aires in a consulting role. Earlier God had shown Himself strong on their behalf, but by the time of my visit, there was little quickening of life and power.

With a Kingdom overlay to guide church life, we will not have a limited vision of what we are privileged to be and do. We start with a Kingdom perspective of being who we are in Christ. That leads to do what Kingdom people do and to do everything as unto Him. The consciousness of Christ in us, which is the true meaning of Christianity, must occur. We do everything as unto Him. He is our focus because He is the light that is giving the focus.

THE KINGDOM IS RECEIVED; THE CHURCH IS BUILT

We do not build the Kingdom, but we receive what is already ours as a result of extravagant grace. We receive what the Lord is sending. The Kingdom comes and all that we must do is receive it. We are the receivers, just as we receive everything in the Christian life. *"As you have received Christ Jesus the Lord, so walk in Him"* (Col. 2:6). He gives; we receive.

The Church is built. We are not the builders. The Lord builds the Church (see Matt. 16:18). As we receive the Kingdom by receiving His life and presence in action, the Church is built.

When we build the Church, we always stop at the city limits of church life. In the Kingdom there are no city limit signs. He is the Lord of everything; He is the "I am" (see Ex 3:14;John 14:6). Church life takes on an entirely new dimension in the Kingdom consciousness of His Lordship. He is not Lord of "our church" alone or our family alone, but of the community, the city, and the nations. Life is not cut up into the secular and the spiritual. Everything has the capacity to be sacred or spiritual because everything was created by Him and for Him.

Chapter 13

GOING BEHIND THE DOOR OF THE CHURCH

The picture of Jesus knocking at the door of the Laodicean church (see Rev. 3:10) is also a picture of portions of the Church today. Whatever is going on behind the closed door, He is not part of.

Martin Luther walked to the door of the Wittenberg church with 95 statements or theses. He took a hammer and nails and placed those truths that were important to him on the door. His hammer was used to alert the Church that there was a better way. He had experienced the Lord through faith.

After walking to Rome as part of his spiritual pilgrimage, Martin Luther was humbly climbing the steps of a church on his knees when the Lord spoke to his heart, *"...The just shall live by faith"* (Rom. 1:17). He got up off of his knees. He suddenly knew that works were not what God wanted, but faith in the completed work of Christ. That experience led him to suggest a better way than the traditions of the Church he loved. God's way was not offering forgiveness of sin through indulgences, but through faith in Christ. Thus, Luther presented 95 concerns and insights.

He did not nail the door of the church shut. He nailed something onto the door. There is a big difference. Nailing shut the door would have meant his rejection of the Church. He did not do that. Later, the Catholic Church rejected him, but he loved the potential of Christ's life being preeminent in that church.

Years ago I spent most of a week with a selected group of men listening to one of the most gifted men I have ever met in my travels of the world. He came from the same heritage as mine. Because of understanding he received and the harsh reactions from many in the structured church, he turned from that form of church life totally. As an advocate of the Church without walls, meeting in houses, he offered his insights. He had nailed shut the door of the structured or institutional church.

Since then, I have met two other men who reached the same conclusion. They would say the Church as we know it is beyond being restored to be the Body of Christ again. One of them I heard just as I was prepared to write this portion of this book. He, too, had nailed shut the door of the contemporary Church.

My own perspective is that Christ is still knocking with a firm, loving hand, asking to join the journey of the Church today. The journey of today's Church is not unlike a journey years ago. That Emmaus road experience is repeated by many who walk with a comparative stranger all day. They talk about Christ. Finally they awaken and discover they were talking *about* Him when they could have been talking *to* Him (see Luke 24:13-31). He is here with us—even within us. He is our companion in this journey. He is here to be enjoyed, and He wants to share His life with us.

It is not time to nail shut the door of the contemporary Church. We do, however, need to nail to the door of this structured church the truth that Jesus would really like to come in. With Him would come the Kingdom. With the Kingdom would come a meaningful experience of church life that we have long called revival and awakening.

There are not many models of church life that come from a Kingdom perspective. Spectator church life is not a Kingdom model. Everyone has great value to the team that assembles around Christ's presence. Everyone becomes a showcase of His life. The gathering in the church building is no more significant than times when the members influence the lives of others in their daily commitments. The real Kingdom action takes place in many locations other than the church building.

The response mechanism of a Kingdom-oriented church is as quick as Christ's response from within the believer. Boards, committees, titles, and control mechanisms are often a bureaucracy offering resistance. Out of the gifts and callings of God, He fashions a coordinated Body. It is His Body evidencing that He is the head with a central nervous system or order that responds to Him. Love is the ruling order of the church when Christ rules.

GOING BEHIND THE DOOR OF THE CHURCH

We must face the fact that not everything that says church is church. One of the revered men who stood out as a preaching model for the English-speaking world was G. Campbell Morgan of Westminster Chapel, London, England. Most pastors of my era have the books of G. Campbell Morgan in their libraries, as I do.

His ultimate successor was Dr. Martin Lloyd-Jones, formerly a physician who was being trained to be the physician to the Royal family of England. The successor of Dr. Lloyd-Jones was Dr. R.T. Kendall. He offers this amazing comment about this trilogy of pastors at Westminster Chapel:

> Dr. Lloyd-Jones often quoted G. Campbell Morgan as saying: "Westminster Chapel is not a church, it is a preaching center." I once asked him, "Doctor, was Westminster Chapel a church in your day?" He paused and took what seemed like a minute to answer: "Just barely" he finally replied.[1]

One famous pastor said that the church he made famous was not really a church, but a preaching center. His equally famous successor said that during his tenure, Westminster Chapel was "just barely" a church.

Tragically, today many so-called churches are not really churches, but centers as well. Others are "just barely" a church. Centers vary from preaching centers, entertainment centers, centers for contemplation (with not much to think about), centers offering insurance for life and death, or even centers to simply hide in while feeling good about yourself.

Athletics and entertainment have probably set the standard for the contemporary American church more than anything else. Without a Kingdom vision, we gravitate to the things we see most. So we are accustomed to paying to watch others play. Most churches are filled with spectators who watch a team play. They are called on to serve on committees, greet the fans at the door, and do countless other jobs to keep the stadium filled and the budget met.

While we meet, we need to ask the question, "Is Christ behind the door with us?" If the crowd is large, it is assumed He must be present and enjoying whatever we are attracted to. In our world of sports mania, an enterprising industry has grown up. Sports figures are marketed as cardboard cut-outs. Though the celebrity is not present, his or her likeness is put into picture form. Now the figure is available in any setting we may choose.

Without the manifest presence of Christ, we create a cardboard likeness. Many graphic techniques can be used today. The synthesizing of music, words, and pictures create an atmosphere of entertainment that makes the time pass enjoyably. A cardboard Christ can fill church services or anywhere else we may chose. But the cardboard Christ will not be present when we leave those places. There will be no "burning hearts" in life's journey so that what we do every day has His companionship and guidance.

With the manifested Christ, however, who said, *"I will be with you always"* (Matt. 28:20), we experience His guided presence. When He stops for "the least of these," we stop with

Him. When He takes on the greatest challenges, we take them on, too. The ability to find what He is doing and doing it with Him can only occur when we are walking with Him. We cannot know what Christ is doing and join Him unless we can see Him, hear Him, and watch what He is doing. If we cannot watch Him because He is left on the other side of the door, how can we join Him? Whatever He is doing is a Kingdom engagement, and we must be part of it.

FROM GLORY TO GLORY

I feel like I am entering a very, very sacred place that deserves walking carefully, speaking quietly, and duly honoring where honor is due. With much thought, which means to me, seeking to let Christ's mind engage mine, I am writing these perspectives. Said another way, "I am carefully praying."

One of the most honest books I have ever read is, *In Pursuit of His Glory* by Dr. R.T. Kendall. Starting with a personal encounter with the glory of Christ's presence and traveling through the academic halls of Oxford, he then traces his 25 years as pastor of Westminster Chapel, London.

His encounter with the glory of God changed his life. His own words punctuate the reality of that encounter:

> On Monday morning, October 31, 1955, driving back to Trevecca Nazarene College in Nashville, I had what I only call a "Damascus Road" experience, although it was not my conversion. I believe it was my baptism in the Holy Spirit. I found myself praying hard with

a very heavy burden and was beginning to wonder if I was saved or sanctified. ...

Suddenly there appeared as if before my very eyes the Lord Jesus Himself, interceding before me at God's right hand. I began to weep with joy as I drove. I found myself becoming a spectator; I was carried into the heavenlies. Jesus was praying for me! I couldn't tell what He was saying, only that I felt such love that I was almost overwhelmed. I still wonder how I was able to drive.

The next thing I remember is forty-five minutes later, just before arriving at Trevecca, when I heard Jesus say to the Father, "He wants it." I heard a voice answer back, "He can have it." In that moment I felt a surge of warmth enter into my chest. I could feel it physically although I am sure it was mainly spiritual. There appeared before me the face of Jesus looking at me with such peaceful eyes. The vision of the Lord Jesus lasted for less than a minute, and then I pulled into the parking lot of Trevecca.

I soon began to have visions. I saw that I would one day have an international ministry—not within the denomination which I had known, for my spiritual experience had changed my theology. For example, I knew I was eternally saved; I even saw that God predestined the elect. I began to be truly convicted of sin and identified with 1 John 1:8 (NIV), *"If we claim to be without sin, we deceive ourselves and the truth is not in us."* I thought I had discovered something "new"—that I was the only person since the apostle Paul to see those things! I experienced a real closeness to the Lord Jesus.[2]

Placing this marvelous experience of R.T. Kendall here does not mean I believe this experience of encountering the glory will be the same for everyone. Nor would Dr. Kendall make this the standard. What is clear in Scripture is that every Christian is to experience the Glory of God.

But we all, with unveiled face, beholding as in a mirror the glory of the Lord, are being transformed into the same image from glory to glory, just as by the Spirit of the Lord (2 Corinthians 3:18).

We all are meant to behold the glory. The glory encounter creates transforming change. Such was true of R.T. Kendall as he saw the completeness of eternal salvation that is ours in Christ. Change occurred almost instantly as well as progressively. The rightful experience is to move from glory to glory. Many times I have moved from glory to remembering. I was remembering the past experience instead of receiving the new one.

This wonderful account of a man ministering in the paragon of excellence in preaching totally captivated me. He honored history in a culture rich with history. Remarkable skills in breaking the bread of the Word of God were evident. From the oven of his warm heart and brilliant mind have come 50 books and countless sermons.

With a Doctorate from Oxford, the honors that come from such an influential church, and association with some of the world's leading people, both spiritually and socially, he never lost a hunger for the glory, or as he phrased it, "revival." No longer living in the glory of Christ's presence that he knew in the account just shared from his book, he did not move from glory to glory, but from glory to remembering past experiences as I have often done.

His pursuit of the glory led him to be open to installments of God's guidance through people who otherwise would probably have never been considered. Cultural walls are high in London. Moving them or tearing them down is not a simple process. Authur Blessitt, whose walk with Christ included carrying a literal cross, was invited to speak at Westminster Chapel, first in a small study group and then in a regular service. From that experience came street witnessing, a concern for the poor, and the breaking down of some formalities.[3]

Then came what Dr. Kendall calls "Tracing the Rainbow Through the Rain" at "the chapel."[4] A greater variety of music was presented, along with numerous speakers. Among those who touched the church was Billy Graham. Dr. Kendall had become a Southern Baptist and was schooled at Southern Baptist Theological Seminary in Louisville, Kentucky, where he earned a Master's of Theology. Billy Graham was his hero, as well as a fellow Baptist. That was not true of some in the church. There was mounting opposition from a group in the church with regard to Billy Graham. Dr. Lloyd-Jones had refused to back the Billy Graham crusades of the past. But R. T. Kendall pushed back against the opposition, and Billy Graham spoke at a Sunday night service for which the building could barely seat the crowd.

An openness to hear those outside his circles came from his pursuit of the glory. Among those he heard was John Wimber, who emphasized signs and wonders. Of that meeting in Westminster Central Hall, Dr. Kendall wrote, "His emphasis on the kingdom of God seemed to cohere with my view. I wrote in my journal: 'Is God leading me in this direction? I should wish so.'"[5]

His openness led to Rodney Howard-Browne being received into his life as well. Through Rodney Howard-Browne and others, the Lord drew both his son and his daughter back to a walk with the Lord.[6] Others in the list of refreshing vessels who influenced "the chapel" and R.T. Kendall included Jack Taylor and Charles Carrin. Later he teamed up with Jack and Charles to do "Word, Spirit, Power" conferences. These conferences were aimed at a balance of teaching the Word of God and letting the presence and power of God confirm that Word.

This honest, humble man, whose degrees from academia are formidable and whose honors from many sources are considerable, never lost his thirst for the glory that filled his car and his life that Monday morning October 31, 1955. His quest for the glory can inspire us to be on a glory alert.

THE CREATOR OF THE GLORY

Moving from glory to glory comes through the Spirit of the Lord. We *are being transformed into the same image from glory to glory, just as by the Spirit of the Lord"* (2 Cor. 3:18). The glory of God is created by the person of God in the Holy Spirit.

Christ's life within us and His manifest presence are created by the Holy Spirit. Jesus made that very clear by sharing what He would pray for us to experience.

> *And I will pray the Father, and He will give you another Helper, that He may abide with you forever—the Spirit of truth, whom the world cannot receive, because it neither sees Him nor knows Him; but you know Him, for He dwells with you and will be in you. I will not leave you orphans; I will come to you. A little while longer and the world will see Me no more, but you will see Me. Because I live, you will live also. At that day you will know that I am in My Father, and you in Me, and I in you* (John 14:16-20).

The Holy Spirit is the promised one whom Jesus called *"another Helper."* The word *another* means one identical to or an exact duplicate of. Some have called the Holy Spirit the other Jesus. Knowing that He is in the Father, we are in Him, and He is in us, all come from the illuminating work of the Holy Spirit. His glory and His presence are Holy Spirit enactments.

This glory is the light by which we see everything relating to the Kingdom of God as well as the Lord's life and presence with us. Our spiritual eyes cannot see until His light comes. Light can't come when the switch is thrown to the off position.

Power that reaches our house will not light the house. The master switch must be turned to the on position.

Paul asked the people at Ephesus, *"Did you receive the Holy Spirit when you believed?"* (Acts 19:2). They hadn't because they didn't know about Him. They had not progressed beyond John's baptism to Jesus either. But the question is still significant. Are we receiving the Holy Spirit?

Stiff-arming or ignoring the Holy Spirit would be like refusing to receive electrical energy. Our farm home where I grew up was lighted and operated from a bank of 32-volt batteries charged from a gas burning Delco generator. When rural electrification came it was a no-brainer to switch to 220 volts supplied from a high line. We never missed the 32-volt level of power in light of the 220 volts. The church has unlimited power available without our attempts at generating a lesser power supply with our gas operated generators.

Unlimited power belongs to Jesus. He said, *"All power and authority is given to Me"* (Matt. 28:18). One of the reasons He stands knocking at the door of the Church is to see if the Holy Spirit's power is turned on. His love for us causes Him to come calling as He did in R.T. Kendall's car. His gift was the Holy Spirit's power. R.T. believed it was his baptism in the Holy Spirit. Whether we call such visitations the baptism of the Spirit or the filling of the Spirit, as I am accustomed to do, receiving the Holy Spirit empowers our life. What we call the experience must not keep us from the Holy Spirit who brings the light and glory to us.

Another description Jesus used for the Holy Spirit is *comforter*. He is not a conspirator who intends to impose in order to embarrass or sidetrack us. He comes bringing exactly what we need. By welcoming the Holy Spirit, we welcome the reign of Christ in our lives. His reigning presence empowers our churches and reaches far beyond. Welcoming the Holy Spirit is part of welcoming Christ's reign and Kingdom presence.

THE CHURCH ON MAIN STREET

A main street location for Kingdom life is coming to the Church. God's Kingdom will not come bypassing church life. In fact, just the opposite will occur. If church life today cannot accommodate Kingdom life, new churches will spring up. Startups are proliferating. Many networks are in place to give guidance to church planting.

A Disney president, Al Weiss, who guides Disney's theme parks both in the United States and internationally, was instrumental in founding Vision 360. He was joined by Bob Roberts of Northwood Church and other leaders experienced in church planting. They envision planting churches in 50 major cities in America and 500 major cities of the world.[7] Al Weiss stated in two settings where I heard him that his greatest excitement is to see the Kingdom of God expanded through church plants. I could not help but reflect on a man managing multiple "Magic Kingdoms" in the Disney Corporation being more excited about God's Kingdom. Such vision is being reported in countless lives.

THE FACE OF THE KINGDOM CHURCH

What will churches that are Kingdom expressions look like? The short answer to that question is—they will look however their builder designs them. Whether there is a redesign of an existing church or a church plant, there are some basic characteristics that need to be present. My own list may not agree with others. That can be healthy. Churches are not to be created out of a copy machine. In fact the copy machine is reducing church life to a mere shadow of reality. Copying other churches' success will not lead to success. They must be created out of a scanner—a scanner that is scanning Heaven and releasing the original of the Lord's design for them. Here are my priorities:

1. *Worship in Spirit and Truth*

Worship does not occur in a building, but in the Spirit. God alone deserves worship. John Piper has wisely said that the highest expression that we give to God is worship.[8] Further, we should do evangelism and missions so that others may experience God in worship. Worship should be seen as a holistic experience that includes a corporate experience, a family experience, and an individual experience. Work is a place for worship as is recreation. Worship in spirit is not limited to a place or an activity.

Truth is a guide for all of life. Truth always leads us to Christ, who is the Truth. Our worship is a consciousness of Him that leads to an exaltation of Him. Truths about Him from Scripture are guides to the truth test of worship. But coded systems of scriptural beliefs were followed carefully by Pharisees who missed the mark and thus missed Christ. Systematic theology will not guarantee truth. Spirit-bathed theology will both honor the written Word and the Living Word. Teaching and preaching that is biblically-based will be a plumb line of a healthy church. That plumb line must combine both Spirit and Truth.

2. *The Bond of Relational Fellowship*

Walking with Christ is walking in the light. Without light, we can't see Him. Without light, we can't see each other. Fellowship starts with Christ and extends to each other.

> *This is the message we have heard from Him and declare to you: God is light; in Him there is no darkness at all. If we claim to have fellowship with Him yet walk in the darkness, we lie and do not live by the truth. But if we walk in the light, as He is in the light, we have fellowship with one another, and the blood of Jesus, His Son, purifies us from all sin* (1 John 1:5-7 NIV).

Relational church life is an essential experience for accountability, encouragement, and nurturing. Small groups foster such bonding, whether through a class and their fellowships or through organized cell group meetings. Isolation makes people easy prey for the enemy. Unity comes in the Spirit with an accompanying bond of peace. Strangers can't exist when a church is experiencing conscious Kingdom fellowship.

Paul encouraged the Philippians to experience Christ's bonding power:

> *If you've gotten anything at all out of following Christ, if His love has made any difference in*

your life, if being in a community of the Spirit means anything to you, if you have a heart, if you care— then do me a favor: Agree with each other, love each other, be deep-spirited friends. Don't push your way to the front; don't sweet-talk your way to the top. Put yourself aside, and help others get ahead. Don't be obsessed with getting your own advantage. Forget yourselves long enough to lend a helping hand.

Think of yourselves the way Christ Jesus thought of Himself. He had equal status with God but didn't think so much of Himself that He had to cling to the advantages of that status no matter what. Not at all! When the time came, He set aside the privileges of deity and took on the status of a slave, became human! Having become human, He stayed human. It was an incredibly humbling process. He didn't claim special privileges. Instead, He lived a selfless, obedient life and then died a selfless, obedient death—and the worst kind of death at that: a crucifixion.

Because of that obedience, God lifted Him high and honored Him far beyond anyone or anything, ever, so that all created beings in heaven and on earth—even those long ago dead and buried—will bow in worship before this Jesus Christ, and call out in praise that

He is the Master of all, to the glorious honor of
God the Father (Philippians 2:1-11 MSG).

Bonding with our fellow Christians becomes a foundational aspect of knowing Christ. We see Him in each other. We learn from Him through each other. We honor Him in each other. We share Him as we share with each other. A study of the "one another's" in Scripture is extensive and invigorating. Here is a short list:

- Teach and admonish one another (see Rom. 15:14).

- Abound in love for one another (see 1 Thess. 3:12).

- Comfort one another (see 1 Thess. 4:18).

- Encourage one another (see Heb. 10:25).

- Pray for one another (see James 5:16).

- Do not speak against one another (see Titus 3:2).

- Do not complain against one another (see Col. 3:13-14).

- Be hospitable to one another (see 1 Peter 4:9)

- Love one another (see 1 John 4:7).

- Remember that there is another. We need each other and others need us (see 1 John 4:12).

3. *Order of Church Structure*

The Body of Christ must have a skeleton. There is a necessary structure to support the rest of the Body. But if the structure becomes the ruling order, instead of the head, then the Body will be spastic and lack coordination. A person with a spinal column injury, whose body has lost signals from the head, cannot be normal. Christ's Body must receive guidance from His mind. Much current church life is ordered by a corporate model instead of the model of God's family functioning with spiritual fathers nurturing people. Jesus gave us a model of organic life flowing from the bottom upward not from the top down. I have seen and been part of committee-led churches and elder-led churches across the years. Neither are coordinated expressions of Christ's body unless Christ is permitted to be the head.

The nation of Israel fell into this subtle trap. They had a king who was invisible, all knowing, and all powerful. His rule created a spiritual order. They wanted a king they could see so they would be like their neighboring nations (see 1 Sam 8:1-22). God wanted to be their king just like Jesus wants to be our king of church life today, acting as our head and sharing His mind in a coordinated body that does greater works than He did (see John 14:12).

The biblical model is an eldership that honors the rule of Christ as undisputed head of His body. Eldership is best when it finds a vehicle for honoring the thoughts of all in the church. People will vote, so a healthy body can include an option to vote. Voting need not be done in business meetings, but on ballots following adequate communication. People vote with their mouths, their presence, and their pocketbooks. Wise is the group that hears God together and lets elders offer recommendations that are affirmed by the ballots of church members.

For 18 years I was part of an eldership at Lake Country Baptist Church, Fort Worth, Texas, that gave honor to Christ in every member. That eldership was in place under the leadership of Dr. T. W. Hunt, Dr. Ernest Byers, M.D., and Bob Mauldin when I arrived. Other elders joined us and we developed a decision-making method that led to a loving way of honoring each other. When major decisions were made such as staff members being called, land being purchased, buildings being built, or the annual budget approved, we communicated the recommended decision. A ballot was distributed that had three entrees: 1. Having prayed about this, I affirm this as God's will. 2. Having prayed about this, I disaffirm this as God's will. 3. Having prayed about this, I don't know. There was a place to sign the ballot with the notation that to sign meant you wanted to meet with the elders. If one person disaffirmed the recommendation with a signed name, they met with the elders to share their reason for the disaffirmation. We did not move forward with the plan until that person was willing to give time to hear the Lord with the other members.

In the 16 years after the plan was implemented, everyone affirmed the recommendation after the first meeting with the elders. Had the person not be in agreement we would have gone back through the same process stating the person's concerns about the decision. After a second ballot and the same unresolved concerns of that person, we would have announced that the person's concerns remained the same, but to honor the rest of the people just as we honored the objecting member, we were implementing the recommendation. Again, in the 16 years of this practice we never had any concerns after the first meeting with the elders. It was not a perfect system but it caused each member to find the mind of Christ just as the elders sought to do. We honored Christ in each other. Government is important, but it is not the glue that holds the church together; only the presence of Christ and His mind expressed is that glue.

4.   *Government Response Capability*

Decision making and the ability to respond to needs is the issue of church government. When Christ was in His individual body, He responded to people and their needs as His Father gave guidance. His corporate Body, the Church, should have a response mechanism that is effective. That requires being highly sensitive to needs and equally alert to the Lord's guidance for meeting them.

When systems become bureaucratic, the response time can drag out indefinitely. When response time is slow, needs may compound several times over. Jesus responded to the request of a Roman centurion immediately. His Body now should be able to discern and respond to genuine needs as quickly.

KINGDOM RESPONSES I JUST WITNESSED

This writing has continued through the Christmas season of 2008. A long-time friend of 30 years, Bud Starnes, invited me to join him in taking gifts to people who are his friends. He owns countless properties, many of which are residences for low-income families in north Fort Worth. I rode with him on Christmas Eve day into many of those neighborhoods. Stories of the Lord leading him to the properties and the people living in them were endless. Well over 125 houses are now owned by the occupants who were able to buy them from him. Many of these houses are free of any debt. Stories of how people found hope and learned skills in money management flowed with excitement from his lips.

We stopped at a home where a mother with seven children lived in a one-room apartment. He gave her a gift of cash to assist with their needs. We stopped at Victory Temple Home for men and visited some of the leaders as he left monies for their needs. It is a home with 74 men, most of whom have been set free from drug addiction. A few blocks away is the home for women that houses 15 to 20 ladies.

We drove to a nursing home to visit Willie, a lady who was a tenant in one of his houses for many years. She is nearly blind and totally deaf and can only move about in a wheelchair. He loved her, wrote notes to her, and left practical gifts to let her know she remains a person of value. All of her life, she made her living by picking up cans. But during that time she was more than a tenant in one of his houses. She was a friend. Though she no longer is able to live there due to her health, her value to him has never changed because of Christ's value for her.

The day before, he had called Mike Doyle of Cornerstone Assistance Network about a family he knew that was in need. Mike is a former professional PGA Golf Tour Player, who plays par at Christian service. The family was about to be evicted from a property not owned by my friend. Since the family had no food and many needs, he wanted to find ways to help them. With regret he said, "I didn't know of a single church that could respond to their need." While Bud was on the phone with Mike Doyle on December 23, Mike took another call from a man who was asking where he could give $500 to help a family. Mike connected him to Bud, and this family had their needs met.

I had spent a good part of that day with a Kingdom man doing what people do when Christ lives His life through them.

Christmas morning I attended a service with my dear friend Howard Caver at the Immanuel's Health Care Nursing Home. It was a great time and a great place to celebrate Christmas. Howard's son, Dimitri Caver, gave an excellent message of hope. Howard shared with the occupants how World Missionary Baptist Church, where he is pastor, gave funds they had planned to use for their building to build this first class facility. He made this comment, "This complex is larger than our church building." Here was a Kingdom engagement done because of a Kingdom man with a vision.

When we are alert to the needs around us—when we are sensitive to the Lord's guidance—we will see Kingdom exploits proliferate around us.

Chapter 14

FACING THE HOLE THING

A Hole in the Eye
A Hole in our Gospel
A Hole in our Hearts

"There is a hole in our gospel!" Richard Stearns has declared in his book, *The Hole in Our Gospel*.[1] Twice I have walked with the CEO of World Vision. The first time was a three-mile walk from village to village in Kerala, South India, many years ago with Bob Pierce, the founder of World Vision. Bob Pierce prayed, "Let my heart be broken by the things that break the heart of God." Out of that prayer World Vision has been a channel for practical Kingdom expressions to reach the poor people of the world.

Recently, I walked with Richard Stearns, the current World Vision president, page by page through his excellent book. He dared to address issues we normally duck. "Our gospel" is not the Gospel Jesus preached or the Gospel of the New Testament. It is a Gospel now full of holes. He was impacted by a friend who, along with his friends, took every book in the Bible that discussed poverty, wealth, justice, and oppression and cut those verses out. Some 2,000 verses deal with poverty and justice. The friend would hold up the mutilated Bible and declare, "This is our American Bible; it is full of holes."

The Bible we believe is the Bible we practice! Religious clichés declare, "I believe every word in the Bible, including the cover, which says 'Genuine Cowhide.' I even believe the maps found in the back." The fact is that what we practice is what we believe. "Our gospel" is not the Gospel that Jesus preached or the Gospel of the New Testament. It is a Gospel now full of holes. We have a Bible with verses and pages cut out from our lack of practice, thus Richard Stearns title *The Hole in Our Gospel*.

Richard Stearns's journey to Christ was marked with much thought, which took him from total skepticism, believing that the life and resurrection of Jesus was no more than an "Easter Bunny Story," to knowing Christ personally. A journey into the corporate world led to success and perks of the affluent, which did not diminish his devotion or faithfulness to Christ. After 23 years of corporate leadership, he was asked to leave the familiar and take the leadership of World Vision. The decision was not easy. Surrendering to the clear call of God led him to see a world of need and neglect. This is a world were people's practical needs often go unnoticed, resulting in needless hardships and often unnecessary deaths.

With vivid colors he paints a word picture of what he believes "our gospel" now looks and sounds like.

We have taken this amazing good news from God, originally presented in high definition and Dolby stereo, and reduced it to a grainy, black-and-white, silent movie. In doing so, we have also stripped it of much of its power to change not only the human heart but also the world.[2]

Recognizing the Kingdom of God as God's operative, eternal plan, Richard declares,

The kingdom of which Christ spoke was one in which the poor, the sick, the grieving, cripples, slaves, women, children, widows, orphans, lepers and aliens—*"the least of these"* (Matt. 25:40 NKJV)—were to be lifted up and embraced by God....His was not a far off and distant kingdom to be experienced only in the afterlife; no, Christ's proclamation of the "kingdom of heaven" was a call for a redeemed world order populated by redeemed people—*now*.[3]

A hole exists in our Gospel because a hole exists in our hearts coming from a hole that exists in our vision. My own account of a macular hole developing in my left eye led to my epiphany in revisiting the issues of Kingdom reality. Lost sight leads to a lost understanding of the basic message of Jesus and the Gospel of the Kingdom. When we lose sight of Jesus, we lose sight of His Kingdom.

When we lose sight of the Kingdom, we lose the fullness of Christ's occupancy in our hearts. The hole in our vision is what creates the hole in the Gospel that we thought we understood. Our lack of understanding leaves a void, a hole in our hearts. Not knowing who we are, we act in ways that contradict the rights belonging to members of God's royal family. A hole in the eye of understanding creates a hole in the Gospel of the Kingdom. We end up with a heart void of security and void of a sense of acceptance in God's beloved family.

THE HOLE IN OUR GOSPEL

Recently, Ed Stetzer pointed out that Jesus spoke of the Kingdom 80 times and of the Church only 2 times.[4] As part of the research department of LifeWay in Nashville, he was pointing out the need for church life to flow from a Kingdom-based perspective. That ratio of 80 to 2 references would be reversed in what most churches today are hearing. We would likely hear about the Church 80 times and the Kingdom 2 times, if at all. Most pastors believe the Church is the Kingdom. If Kingdom teaching occurs, it usually is defined as missions beyond the church property or the church neighborhood, and it more often requires a passport for travel to another nation.

How did our Gospel develop such a large hole that something so sizable as the Kingdom could fall through? It would be presumptuous of me to assume I can answer that question better than you can. While I may not know how the hole that has caused the Kingdom to slide from our consciousness was torn, I am certain that a gaping hole does exist in the Gospel most people hear across America each Sunday.

Instead of declaring the Gospel of the Kingdom, we have been declaring the "Gospel of salvation," which offers the right for people to go to Heaven. That message is "How to let Jesus in." Letting Him in gives the receiver the right to go to Heaven. An insurance policy is offered, with the dues already paid. Going to Heaven is the goal. The Gospel of the Kingdom includes going to Heaven, but offers a relationship with the living God as a member of His family doing the business of the family on earth.

The Gospel of the Kingdom, in contrast to a "Gospel of salvation," not only includes letting Christ in but also letting Him out. Going to Heaven is a benefit, but the greater reality is Heaven coming to us here—now! Kingdom coming realities were the offer of Jesus. When the Kingdom of God's plan for all of time and eternity is enacted, the will of God is done on earth as it is in Heaven. Jesus made being born again a necessity, not an option. But His emphasis was not on going to Heaven, but on *"entering"* and *"seeing"* the Kingdom (see John 3:3,5).

A favorite message, probably heard more than any other, is the "gospel of successful church." A successful life is offered as part of this success standard. Feeling good about self leads to good family life, good careers, and the realization of the American dream; that is at the heart of this message. "Nothing succeeds like success" would be a likely theme of this message.

Successful church for most of America is akin to following a business or corporate model that speaks of success numerically and financially. Large numbers of people at church mean "we must be doing something right." With people come dollars. Dollars allow us to make the building where we meet larger or more attractive. The cycle of more people, more dollars, and better buildings becomes endless. Buildings are often thought of as God's house. Building God a better house is a mark of prestige. Sadly, the house where many think He lives is not His house at all. His dwelling place is not in temples made with hands, but in lives who have welcomed His ruling order (see Acts 17:24-25). God will only be present when people who house His presence enter that building. Empty church buildings do not house God. He is found in the hearts that have become His home.

I have already placed emphasis on the fact that Jesus is often standing outside the door of the Church knocking, as seen in a passage usually misapplied. Part of His message to the church at Laodicea was *"Behold, I stand at the door and knock. If anyone hears My voice and opens the door, I will come in to him and dine with him, and he with Me"* (Rev. 3:20). That verse has long been taken from its original context, as a message to a church, and made into an evangelistic appeal. We forget what door Jesus was knocking on and why He was knocking. He was knocking on the door of a church because He was outside and not part of their activities. Whatever was going on, however meaningful it was to them, He was not a part of. It is hard to face that possibility existing in the churches we are part of and love. But facing it is mandatory if we want Jesus on the other side of the door with us.

To the door of the Church in history, Martin Luther nailed his concerns. He believed Jesus was outside the door with him, wanting in. Again, for emphasis, I repeat that he did not nail the door shut. It was not in his heart to write the Church off as a lost cause. His heart called for transformation and a return to

Christ without the layers of tradition and baggage that did not contain the way, the truth, and the life of Christ.

Many today are nailing the door shut. George Barna has pointed out the thousands of Christians who walk out of churches each year.[5] They chose instead to follow Jesus in isolation from church as they know it. Better to nail to the door the issues we know need consideration, as Richard Stearns has so effectively done, than to walk away. Along with nailing up the issues we know we must face, we also need to stand with Jesus and knock with love and persistence. Nailing our concerns to the door and going no farther is not much better than nailing the door shut. Knocking as Jesus knocks means we want to be part. His knock is a call for transformation. Reformation was a start, yet transformation still awaits the Church. Only our minds being renewed (when His mind is received in us) will bring this transformation. Our fragmented Gospel can be glued back quickly when we truly receive the mind of Christ.

THE HOLE IN OUR HEARTS

Jesus came to fill the hole in our hearts. Our hearts cry out for love and acceptance. Adam was the first son of God who knew the Father's total love and fellowship. The first son of God forfeited his relationship as a son. But God's love found a way to offer His only begotten Son. This Son, Jesus, would restore, through the cross and the resurrection, the reality of His life within us and the fellowship with the Father that Adam lost.

Adam's brilliant mind was greatly damaged when he believed the lie that eating from the tree of knowledge would make him like God. He was already like Him. But like a drug that blows the mind, his sin blew his thinking into a complete distortion of reality. He then saw Himself naked and ashamed. He was no more naked than at the time of creation, but he began to see himself as naked. Adam was a spirit clothed with a body. So, he was already clothed. God asked him, *"Who told you that you are naked?"* (Gen. 3:11). Adam's faulty thinking clouded every response. His Father came to him, but he did not see him as a Father coming with love. He feared that He was coming in retribution. So he hid from Him. Perfect love casts out all fear (see 1 John 4:18). Imperfect fear pushes back against love's advance.

Instead of seeing himself a son, his mind recorded the conclusion that he was an orphan. God had made a son. Adam made a decision that resulted in the first orphan. Now with an orphan mind, no longer thinking with the clarity of a son, Adam felt alone and undone. A Father was no longer his provider, protector, and pleasure. Instead of letting the Father provide for him, he engaged in providing his own clothes. Instead of wanting the Father's fellowship, he hid in fear and dread.

It was the worst swap that ever occurred. Adam swapped being a son for being an orphan. With that He swapped the spiritual for the carnal, the eternal for the temporary, and knowing God for wanting to know God. Religion was introduced to the human family instead of a relationship with God as a Father. Doing things for God instead of allowing God to provide was the difference.

Jesus came as the only begotten Son of God to restore all who receive Him to their original position as children of God (see John 1:14). The Gospel of Jesus Christ is a Gospel that restores the relationship the first son of God, Adam, had with the Father. Contained in this genderless sonship, every daughter has the same restoration. The only begotten Son of God creates the restored rights of sonship for every believer.

That is why Jesus declared, *"I will not leave you as orphans; I will come to you"* (John 14:18 NIV). His declaration of that truth could not be more clear.

> *If you love Me, you will obey what I command. And I will ask the Father, and He will give you another Counselor to be with you forever—the Spirit of truth. The world cannot accept Him, because it neither sees Him nor knows Him. But you know Him, for He lives with you and will be in you. I will not leave you as orphans; I will come to you. Before long, the world will not see Me anymore, but you will see Me. Because I live, you also will live. On that day you will realize that I am in My Father, and you are in Me, and I am in you. Whoever has My commands and obeys them, he is the one who loves Me. He who loves Me will be loved by My Father, and I too will love him and show Myself to him* (John 14:15-21 NIV).

Since Jesus declared He was not going to leave us as orphans, the question remains, "Why are we victimized with this kind of thinking?" Obviously, we were not left as orphans by Jesus. Instead, our orphan thinking occurs because we don't know that we were placed in Christ and that Christ was placed in us so that we can enjoy full sonship. Or we may know it, but do not believe it because our orphan thought patterns reject it. We may believe our experience more than the fact of God's Word. Feelings of rejection and incompletion may dominate our thinking if we don't take our thoughts captive and in faith receive our acceptance into the family as joint heirs with Christ.

My own journey in realizing "who I am in Christ" was a major breakthrough, as I described previously. Even more important was the realization that an orphan mentality continued to reject portions of the reality of my identification in Christ. Without transformed minds, our thoughts take us captive instead of us taking every thought captive (see Rom. 12:2, 2 Cor. 10:5). This is an essential element in seeing and enjoying the Kingdom privileges and endeavors of a child of God.

There are many characteristics of orphan mentality, but three major issues are uppermost in the mind of an orphan.

1. *Provision Becomes an Obsession*

Enough is never enough for an orphan. An orphan never feels complete and never has enough. An acquaintance of mine grew up in the Kennedy Compound in Florida. As a young man, he had an unguarded conversation with Joseph P. Kennedy, the patriarch of this famous family. "Mr. Kennedy how much money does it take to satisfy a man?" was his youthful inquiry. "Just a little bit more," was the honest reply of the aged mega-millionaire. That is classic orphan thinking. A little bit more is always necessary for the orphan mind because orphans don't see themselves as endowed.

Jesus declared in graphic language that we can find models in birds and lilies that our Father will care for us. The birds know it; the lilies experience it without even the need of knowing it. So far as I know, lilies don't engage in cognitive processes. It's amazing that Jesus would use lilies as an example when they aren't even engaged in planning and preparing (see Matt. 6:25-30).

His point was this:

> *So do not worry, saying, "What shall we eat?" or "What shall we drink?" or "What shall we wear?" For the pagans run after all these things, and your heavenly Father knows that you need them. But seek first His kingdom and His righteousness, and all these things will be given to you as well. Therefore do not worry about tomorrow, for tomorrow will worry about itself. Each day has enough trouble of its own* (Matthew 6:31-34 NIV).

2. Protection Is a Continuous Concern

Orphans, in their insecure mind-set, not only conclude that there is never enough, but also that what they have is never safe. They feel a burning need to protect themselves and their possessions, no matter how meager. They cannot see their Father as their protector, and they refuse to risk personal rejection, loss, or even discomfort. Contrast that with Paul's willingness, as a son, to experience the loss of all things because of what he had gained in Christ.

> *What is more, I consider everything a loss compared to the surpassing greatness of knowing Christ Jesus my Lord, for whose sake I have lost all things. I consider them rubbish, that I may gain Christ and be found in Him, not having a righteousness of my own that comes from the law, but that which is through faith in Christ—the righteousness that comes from God and is by faith* (Philippians 3:8-9 NIV).

All he was and had were considered "rubbish" compared to what he found in Christ. Adam swapped sonship and gained orphan status. Paul swapped orphan status and gained sonship. The swap took place at the cross when Christ swapped out being God's son for being made sin, though He knew no sin (see 2 Cor. 5:21...). With that unimaginable alteration, Jesus became an orphan crying out *"My God, My God why have you forsaken me?"* (Matt. 27:46). Through His decision to be made sin for us, we have been made righteous and now bear the image of God's workmanship as a masterful new creation (see Eph. 2:10). Paul knew that, in the cross and resurrection of Christ, everything that belongs to God is returned to us if we enter into our place in Christ through faith.

3. *Position (Title or Role) Holds Great Importance*

The issue for a son is not position but purpose. An orphan loses sight of purpose because of the need for position. Our purpose is the same as the purpose of Jesus, to display the glory of the Father. As sons and daughters, we have the same relationship with the Father that Jesus had while on this earth. Sons and daughters know their position in Christ, and through Christ they receive the same relationship that He had with the Father, which is the highest position that can ever be enjoyed. They have no need for positions, titles, or roles—they are sons and daughters!

The prayer time that Jesus had with His Father deserves to be attended often. In John 17, Jesus lets us pray with Him. Here is significant part of that prayer:

> *I have given them the glory that You gave Me, that they may be one as We are one: I in them and You in Me. May they be brought to complete unity to let the world know that You sent Me and have loved them even as You have loved Me* (John 17:22-23 NIV).

Jesus was here displaying the glory of the Father. He gives us the same purpose because the Father was in Him. Now Jesus is in us, thus bringing the Father's love and purpose to us. We are His brothers and sisters on assignment from and with the Father.

Moving back to Fort Worth has linked me with many old friends. One of my business leader friends was noticeably more relaxed, confident, and full of assurance. A conversation I had with him, while writing this portion of the book, included a discussion of our journeys in learning the meaning of being a son of God, as compared to being an orphan. He shared that his brother's death was the turning point for him. He was named the executor of his brother's estate. While reading the will and performing his duties as executor, he was led by the

Lord to go back and study the Father's Will and Testament written in Scriptures. Realizing that he was in His Heavenly Father's will, he read,

> *Because those who are led by the Spirit of God are sons of God. For you did not receive a spirit that makes you a slave again to fear, but you received the Spirit of sonship. And by Him we cry, "Abba, Father." The Spirit Himself testifies with our spirit that we are God's children. Now if we are children, then we are heirs—heirs of God and co-heirs with Christ, if indeed we share in His sufferings in order that we may also share in His glory* (Romans 8:14-17 NIV).

He saw himself a son and thus an heir with Christ, not only of sonship, but also all of the Father's estate. With a smile born out of a deep faith and the peace of God ruling his life, he said, "I realized I did not need to ask for what was mine. So, I just started thanking Him for what He has chosen to share with me."

Paul knew this transforming truth. He interchanged the term *orphan* with the term *slave*. Paul's transformation included learning that sonship is at the center of our relationship to God and the enactment of His Kingdom.

In addition to the truth in Romans 8 that my friend claimed, Paul wrote the same truth to the Galatians:

> *Because you are sons, God sent the Spirit of His Son into our hearts, the Spirit who calls*

out, "Abba, Father." So you are no longer a
slave, but a son; and since you are a son, God
has made you also an heir (Galatians 4:6-7).

God's children are heirs. What God has, we have. Christ won that right, and the testament or will has been documented. Now it is our right to believe it and enter into the relationship that we have as children. As children of the king, we are kings and priests just as Jesus was. Our Father is King of Heaven and earth. We have been birthed into the royal family to reign in life in Christ Jesus and to serve in life as He served in a priestly role.

Orphans are already saying, "This is too good to be true; you are going too far." Sons are saying, "It is better than you are declaring it, Jim. Raise it on up to the highest level of the rights we were given in the will executed through the death of Christ." The power of words will not convince you of the Father's full benefits to you, His child. But the Holy Spirit's words, heard in your heart, speaking out the loving adoration of "Abba Father," will silence the fears of "this is too much" and will tune in the "much more" that belongs to you.

The orphan mind is the norm in the dysfunctional family of God today called the Church. We have been trained to think and act like orphans. We are not performing to please God, we are participating as members of the family through faith. Sunday events are not our goal but exhibiting God's love and power every day in every engagement is our privilege. Without knowing the implications of orphan thought, we are schooled in how to maintain an effective, functional orphanage. Orphans learn the system of survival. Protection is of uttermost consideration, and the status quo of the orphanage environment is manageable and nonthreatening. Thus, terms like *transformation* are threatening.

The Gospel of the Kingdom is not a teaching or a system. Those who can declare the theology of the Kingdom as a system of teaching without the manifest presence of Jesus are only offering another system that is lifeless. At the heart of the reality of the Kingdom of God is the presence of the King who came to disclose Himself as being *"Our Father who is in heaven"* (Matt. 6:9). Such a linkage of Heaven and earth is a linkage of God's love being exhibited and experienced in a family. It is God's family doing family business on earth in the manner that God intended as He created a world order. That order was a family living in their security and acceptance from Him.

THE WALLS INSIDE ARE THE THICKEST

"Jim, here is a book that will speak to you," said Bob Roberts as he thrust the book *Organic Leadership* by Neil Cole into my hand. As I began to read it that night, I learned why Bob Roberts had written an endorsement of it and was urging me to glean from it.

I plowed into it. Neil Cole offered insights into leadership that caused my own experiences and concerns about church leadership today to lead me to a near sleepless night. One of the gripping realities was his example of the church from the book and movie *The Shawshank Redemption*.

Though not a movie-goer, I had stumbled into that movie years ago as a television feature. For some reason, channel surfing led me to see it again three or four times. That is unheard of for me. I was captivated by the institutional world and the walls around the men, but especially the walls inside them.

The two men in the movie that carry the story line are Andy and Red. Red was the guy who handled all of the contraband of the prison. He was the guy who could get almost anything for the other prisoners. But he had become institutionalized and was fearful about whether he would be able to function outside the walls.

Andy was behind the walls, but was free where freedom always exists, if chosen, in the heart. Though abused and penalized by the corrupted prison system, stemming from a dishonest Warden, Andy remained free. In solitary confinement, Andy was free. In the corridors of his mind, he maintained his freedom. He mastered the system of the prison, but his mastery was aimed at freedom.

As the two men talked about their future, Red declared that he was resigned to staying there until his beard was white and his mind was dulled. Andy declared that he planned to go free and settle on the shores of the Pacific in Mexico. The Mexicans had told him that the Pacific was a place that had no memory. A warm place with no memory was the place Andy envisioned living.

Andy did escape the walls of the prison. The dreaded parole was also given to Red. Freedom was almost more than he could handle, but he chose to follow Andy's instructions, and the closing scene of the movie is the shoreline of the Pacific, a place with no memory, with Red walking toward the waiting Andy.

Neil Cole provides a powerful insight in comparing institutional church life to the institutionalization that take place in a prison.

> It's not a question of whether you are inside the walls, but are the walls inside you? The actual walls of the institution, whether they are brick and mortar or bureaucratic channels and political process, are not the real problem.... A leader must be free if he or she is to lead others to freedom. Some, who remain behind the walls of the institution, can still be free in their minds. Others, outside the institution, may still be captive. Often we get confused and blame the institution, when it is our own mind-set that is really the issue.[6]

With accurate clarity, Neil Cole describes our failed systems:

> The church in the West functions in a pattern similar to that of a dysfunctional relationship. It is locked up in an unhealthy cycle in which the Christian leaders and the regular Christians are codependents. The Christians who are not the church leaders prefer not to take responsibility for the kingdom of God. They want to be free to invest in their own plans rather than God's. They are the irresponsible part in the dysfunctional relationship. ...The

Christian leaders, on the other hand, want to be responsible—to a fault. They continue to do all the work of the church, which enables other Christians to be irresponsible. Leaders need to be needed and admired, and often this is the result when they take all the responsibility for kingdom work. People place them on a pedestal because of the important things they do. Thus a cycle develops.[7]

When the heart is freed with the reality of the Father and Son relationship, leaders and members of churches alike will convert an institutional fortress into a household experience of God's family functioning as designed. This Kingdom reality of a King and His family will create church life that reflects the transformation of being a new creation, God's own child.

When Richard Stearns faced the issue of becoming president of World Vision, he dealt with the discomforts of leaving the systems of the corporate world where he excelled. It was such a traumatic experience that he devotes an entire chapter to discussing the process. With graphic detail he describes returning from a meeting with leaders at World Vision and being so emotionally distraught that he went to bed at four in the afternoon and pulled the covers over his head and wept. His teenage son heard him weeping and came to comfort him. Not unlike Red in the *Shawshank Redemption,* or like an orphan in an orphanage, he found the position that he had mastered now held him captive.[8]

When the sound of God's voice reaches our ears, we find a desire to live in freedom, but at the same time, our fear of the unknown, our possible lack of funds, or our weakness in the skill sets needed to accomplish the task intimidate us. Though Richard Stearns took a 75 percent pay cut, his primary concern was the possibility of not being qualified for the job. Freedom is ours in Christ. Exercising it is the issue. *"It is for freedom that Christ has set us free. Stand firm, then, and do not let yourselves be burdened again by a yoke of slavery"* (Gal. 5:1 NIV). We have freedom, but if we do not exercise it, we see life from the iron bars of our own minds.

THE PAPER WALLS OF MONEY

"Haves" and "have-nots" make up the population of this world. "Haves" can be "have-nots" and "have-nots" can be "haves," depending on how they see themselves. What we have or don't have in worth and assets is recorded between our ears, not on financial spreadsheets. Greed rules the heart that is not ruled by Christ. For that reason, poverty is the king in most of the world. Distribution of wealth breaks down because the "haves" are controlled by a need to horde or to splurge. "Have nots" are ruled by a willingness to settle for mediocrity. Inadequacy comes from the minds of orphans who do not embrace the liberation of Kingdom benefits. Orphans may be rich, but will hold on to that wealth as their security blanket. Orphans who are poor are resigned to cope with poverty as their lot in life and may hold on to their poverty as a type of security as well.

Two men have become the poster boys of this principle in Fort Worth. A book bearing an unusual title, *Same Kind of Different as Me,* gives a riveting account of men so different and yet so much the same. One was born in abject poverty in Louisiana and endured that lot in life for most of his life. The other was born with average wealth, but through the privilege of schooling at Texas Christian University and the right connections in the world of art, he became rich.

With a lifestyle that was not that different from his ancestors, who were slaves, Denver Moore lived on a cotton plantation in Louisiana. Laws said he was freed in the emancipation proclamation paid for by the blood of those who died for his freedom. Experience told him the shack he lived in, the supplies he gained from the plantation store, and the limited skills he knew as a sharecropper farmer left him with nothing more than a day-to-day existence. As an illiterate, he never knew how much he made, how much he owed the plantation store, or what rights really belonged to him.

After years of such an existence, he raised his head in hope to consider that others of his race had better conditions than he knew. He left the plantation and headed as a hitch hiker to California. He got as far as Fort Worth and became a resident living in a card board box on the street.

On another street in Fort Worth, one that was like another world from the street downtown, lived a couple who had met at TCU and later married. With skills in recognizing art masterpieces and knowledge about marketing opportunities, Ron Hall had become a man of wealth. He and his wife, Deborah, became Christians. Deborah wanted to give back some of the blessing they had received. She was led to the Union Gospel mission downtown. Ron struggled to join her in a world so different from their normal experience, but he did.

Though not familiar with the Lord's ability to speak to His children, Deborah Hall had a very graphic dream about a black man who would come through the food line at the Union Gospel Mission. This man she believed would influence the city. She shared the dream with Ron and asked that he be ready to meet the man. Many trips to the mission passed before the man appeared in the food line. It was Denver Moore. He was now a hardened street person who was angry and considered dangerous if provoked. Some of his behavior had led to prison time.

Deborah alerted Ron, "That is the man I saw in the dream." Ron approached a sullen man who refused to talk and wouldn't even give him his name. Someone told Ron that his name was Dallas. So, again and again, he would approach a man he believed was Dallas, but was rebuffed. Finally, at a mission-sponsored event, Denver broke his silence and told Ron his real name.

This compelling story led to two families knowing, loving, and caring for one another. Denver came to know Christ as well. A black man and white man, a poor man and a rich man, became friends. After Deborah's death, Denver Moore moved into the beautiful, upscale home of Ron Hall. He learned to read; He learned to paint. He learned to be who he was always intended to be by a loving Heavenly Father.

They were both poor—only one knew it. They both were rich in Christ, and both of them came to know it. Both enjoyed the love and benefits of their Father. Their "same kind of different" is the same kind that belongs to everyone. Denver Moore demonstrated that our differences have more similarities than we know. Our differences as orphans are really very similar. Our similarities as sons are really the similarities that occur because our Father sees us as being like Jesus, with full acceptance and rights from the Him.[9]

Jesus described how to break out of our bondage to money as he gave the Kingdom issues and operatives on a mountain side. Woven into the liberating truths, He declared that money was not to be our master. Instead we are to master money (see Matt. 6:24).

One pastor I have read knew Kingdom operatives, but did not know Kingdom economics. Aware of this lack, he asked the Lord for insight. He began a study of Jesus' teaching about money. The investment story Jesus told in Matthew 25:14, about a wealthy man who entrusted his servants with money, was the tipping point for him. Jesus said that the Kingdom of Heaven is like a man giving three servants money. In the vernacular of our language, one got $5,000, one got $2,000, and the third got $1,000. The first two invested and doubled their amounts. The third took the $1,000 and guarded it. When their master returned, the first returned the $10,000 he now possessed. The second servant brought the $4,000 he had. The third returned the $1,000 he had been given, offering an explanation for his caution, saying that he not gained anything, but neither had he lost anything. Jesus said that the master was furious and told him to give his amount to the one who had earned the most.

Three principles are clear from this story. We are to multiply money and not spend it. We are to retain a portion of all we get in savings. We are to invest God's gifts to us so that a multiplying process can occur.

The pastor, I read, had a personal breakthrough. His church was soon in a position to do more for others than ever before. Members of the church learned the same principles and became instruments for enabling others. The Kingdom message of economic freedom is not the message of a "prosperity gospel." In fact, it is almost the opposite; while giving is part of the Kingdom message, the primary reality is about saving and investing. Our investment is more than wise financial investment. It is investment in the greatest agency of the Kingdom, namely people who become disciples.

America has learned that our house of financial cards was a failed system. Where our national debt and our shaky financial system will go is far from settled at this writing. But in reality, with our Father's wealth and limitless provisions, we Kingdom believers can be confident. *"His divine power has given us everything we need for life and godliness through our knowledge of Him who called us by His own glory and goodness"* (2 Pet. 1:3 NIV). Part of our knowledge of Him is knowing that we are not orphans left to fend for ourselves. We are His children who are heirs of His entire holdings.

The obscurity of the magnitude of Kingdom implications cannot exist much longer. What God has given us through our family relationship, which is the heart of His Kingdom, will be a demonstration of God's power and life not seen since the days of the early church. Exploits of the early Church were not dependent on the economy or the culture of the country where the good news was declared and demonstrated. The same will be true for us. The silence with regard to the truth of His Kingdom coming is about to be interrupted with preaching and teaching of the message Jesus gave us to experience and share.

The Kingdom of God has never looked so good. Never has sonship been so inviting. A revolution in thinking is occurring.

I am part of a study group in one of the highest per-capita income groups in America. Over the past year, most of these men have walked out of their personal orphanage to find inner confidence in being sons of God. With that confidence has come the assurance that, though many of the economic foundations they were counting on have either been destroyed or greatly reduced, they are secure in the Father's provisions. The faces of these men reflect their confidence and inner certainty that God is faithful. They have been a joy for me to walk with and learn from.

The words of Maltbie D. Babock in a familiar hymn declare the truth of this world's ownership:

THIS IS MY FATHER'S WORLD

This is my Father's world,
and to my listening ears

All nature sings, and round me
rings the music of the spheres.

This is my Father's world:
I rest me in the thought

Of rocks and trees, of skies and seas;
His hand the wonders wrought.

This is my Father's world,
the birds their carols raise,

The morning light, the lily white,
declare their Maker's praise.

This is my Father's world:
He shines in all that's fair;

In the rustling grass I hear Him pass;
He speaks to me everywhere.

This is my Father's world.

O let me ne'er forget
That though the wrong seems oft
so strong, God is the ruler yet.

This is my Father's world:
why should my heart be sad?

The Lord is King; let the heavens ring!

God reigns; let the earth be glad![10]

Chapter 15

THE CHURCH WITH
A FULL HEART

Coming to this last chapter is like coming to the end of a marathon. I have sought to run this race looking unto Jesus, the author and finisher of faith. Several times in this writing His presence has caused me to sit at this computer keyboard and weep. Some of my tears fell as I sensed Him standing with me and weeping, just as He once did over a very religious city (see Luke 19:41). Reviewing our "religious cities" of church life brings tears to my eyes and, I perceive, to the Lord's as well.

Some of my thoughts and conclusions I have "road tested" in teaching forums and with friends while writing. Each time His presence has come to verify these suppositions. I want to be a vessel of His presence through these thoughts and words so that He will visit you. It is my utmost desire that His presence has come or will yet come to visit you in your reading.

Seeing is not believing, but seeing can lead to believing if we chose to believe. My desire to see the Kingdom has increased over the past several years and seems to have reached a crescendo during this past year. How many people have a dissatisfaction with business as usual? I do not know. But those in my circle of acquaintances all seem to have leaned forward with a new anticipation. Something greater than we have ever seen is about to occur. It is my conclusion that we are taking a new look at the Master Plan the Lord has laid out. Glimpses of Kingdom life are taking place.

A summary of my conclusions and desires are found in a prayer of Paul. He was a seer like none other. From the scope of heavenly places to the trenches where he was assaulted and left for dead, he saw Christ. His prayer life reflects this big screen projection of reality:

> *For this reason I bow my knees to the Father of our Lord Jesus Christ, from whom the whole family in heaven and earth is named, that He would grant you, according to the riches of His glory, to be strengthened with might through His Spirit in the inner man, that Christ may dwell in your hearts through faith; that you, being rooted and grounded in love, may be able to comprehend with all the saints what is the width and length and depth and height—to know the love of Christ which passes knowledge; that you may be filled with*

all the fullness of God. Now to Him who is able to do exceedingly abundantly above all that we ask or think, according to the power that works in us, to Him be glory in the church by Christ Jesus to all generations, forever and ever (Ephesians 3:14-21).

He envisioned a Church with a full heart. Christ fills the heart.

- A Christ-filled heart creates a family tie to both Heaven and earth.

- A Christ-filled heart is a Holy Spirit-strengthened heart.

- A Christ-filled heart is filled with all the dimensions of Christ's love.

- A Christ-filled heart is filled with the very fullness of God.

- A Christ-filled heart will give evidence of God's glory in the Church forever.

A more comprehensive coverage in prayer will not be found. This prayer is calling for a Christ-filled heart. Every heart is full of something. What spills when we are jostled reveals what we are filled with.

When the Holy Spirit was welcomed to do a greater work in the later 1960s and early 1970s, Peter Lord of Park Avenue Baptist Church, Titusville, Florida, suggested we needed a magazine to give coverage of His activities. Peter also offered a name given to him by Leonard Ravenhill. It should be called *Fulness,* he suggested.

Fulness magazine was birthed in March 1978 and published for ten years. It made a significant contribution as a teaching instrument and a reporting device of what the Lord was doing. Ras Robinson accepted leadership as president and editor. I was part of the group of leaders who contributed to the reporting and writing.

If I was birthing such a communication tool today, it would be called, *Skyline: Where Heaven Touches Earth.* Truly, we do need such a communication tool to chronicle the many stories of the Kingdom coming to cities across America and the nations of the world. Stories abound, but the reporting vehicle is not in place. Church life stands at a crossroads in America. Many parts of the world now offer models of experiences that have no explanation apart from Christ's life being enacted again. With hearts full of Christ's presence, they allow Him to touch others through them.

HALF-FILLED HEARTS CAN BE FILLED FULL

Paul addressed a church in Galatia that had fallen below the fullness of Christ's life in them. Grace was there as an offering to them, but they fell below it. They were bewitched, Paul declared. Judaizers came with convincing words that they should add to Christ their Jewish rituals and observances again. They were going back to bondage.

Bondage was not only the system they embraced, but demonic deception, Paul told them. It is shocking to our culture that good ideas with deep-seated tradition can actually contain a demonic net to capture us. Galatians 2:9 in the RSV makes this unmistakably clear,

> *Formerly, when you did not know God, you were in bondage to beings that by nature are not god; but now that you have come to know God, or rather to be known by God, how can you turn back again to the weak and beggarly elemental spirits, whose slaves you want to be again?*

These "elemental spirits" are demonic spirits using their skills of disguise to entrap.

Paul was not giving an inch. He would not stand by and watch people get into the trap of substituting self-righteous systems for Christ, as was taught by the Judaizers. Satan does not care if we keep the commandments if we will take the credit for it. Going to church, teaching the Bible, preaching, contending for justice, or doing service projects will not offend satan as long we take credit and do it with our skills. Paul was saying (in paraphrase) "If you go back to that bondage, you will have to do it over my live body." (I say "live body" because Paul was taking a living stance and would not compromise.)

Paul drew another line in the sand in Galatians. Either we are in the Spirit or in the flesh. The flesh is an enemy of God. So even when we think we are God's friends, we may be so subversive that we are actually enemies (see Gal. 5:16-21). It's strong language, I know, but we can't ask God for a rewrite. Paul wrote what he was told to write. For our own sakes, as well as the sake of countless others, we need to get it right.

Paul was not giving up; neither can we! He found hope for the half-filled heart. In intercession likened to labor pains, he wrote that he would "push for them" until Christ was formed in them. As a woman puts her own life on the line to give birth to her child, Paul was saying, "I will put my own life on the line for your heart to be filled."

Christ-filled hearts create Christ-filled churches. Many churches are filled with people. Not all are filled with Christ. The evidence of a heart filled with Christ is found in what comes from that heart everyday in contrast to only on Sunday.

SEEKING CHURCH OR KINGDOM?

Never did Jesus say we are to seek first the Church. He started with the Kingdom as a model to us. Had Jesus announced, "The Church is at hand," there might be a case for our majoring on what He minored on. Kingdom expressions will make church life what He desires the Church to be, His Body touching people.

Some will say, and perhaps as a reader you have already said, "But where does it say Jesus loved the Kingdom and gave Himself for it? It does say, *"...Christ also loved the church and gave Himself for her"* (Eph. 5:25). Indeed, as Ephesians makes clear, Christ was sharing His life with His Church as a bride in the way husbands and wives shares their lives. In the giving of love, there is an intimacy pictured with Christ and His Church.

His Kingdom is not His Body. His Kingdom is His domain or sphere of authority. The best technical definition of the

Kingdom that I know of is the definition of Dr. Gene Mims in his book, *Thine Is The Kingdom:* "The kingdom of God is the reign of God through Jesus Christ in the lives of persons as evidenced by God's activity in and through and around them."[1]

His Kingdom is His life enacted in every sphere. His Church is His Body expressing Him to others. The enactment of His life in Kingdom expressions may include His Body both declaring and manifesting His power, but is not limited to His authority in the Church. His Kingdom touches justice, government, economics, education, medicine, art, entertainment, or any realm that influences people and culture.

The world turned upside down by the early Church included every infrastructure of society. Kingdom engagement does not know separation of Kingdom and state. There are no off-limits places to the lordship or reign of Christ.

Jesus started with the Kingdom and went to the Church. He did not leave the Kingdom in favor of the Church. Instead, He took Kingdom life into Church life. Church was not a place to attend, but an expression of Kingdom life in a functioning Body coordinated by Christ the head. His reign in the Kingdom must be extended to His reign in the Church or the church is not His Body. Without His reign, it becomes a "center," as described in another chapter, or "barely a church." His Kingdom will not come without His reigning presence. Church, as we know it, can occur weekly without His reigning presence.

A KINGDOM SIGHTING 110 YEARS AGO

Insights shared 110 years ago by George Dana Boardman are as relevant today as those being published this year. He saw the Kingdom because he saw Christ. His book *The Kingdom* is a book that I both read and found reading me at the same time.[2]

Paradigms are often adjusted in another culture. Boardman lived outside our culture as a boy. He was the son of missionary parents and was born in Burma. After his father died, his mother married Adoniarm Judson, the famous missionary.

E. Stanley Jones classic book, *The Unshakable Kingdom and the Unchanging Christ,* might never have been written except for his years in India and a look beyond our culture. Bertha Smith's sharp perception of a Christian's true identity might not have occurred had she not studied Scripture in China without commentaries to guide her.

George Boardman pastored the First Baptist Church of Philadelphia, Pennsylvania, from 1864 to 1894. With brilliance as a scholar and thoroughness as a teacher, he develops the scope of Kingdom purpose and life. There is no book that I know that honors Christ and affirms His Kingdom more than this ageless classic. One of his salient statements on the subject of Kingdom engagements and church order is this:

> The keys which our King promised to Peter were not the keys of the church, or the ecclesiastical "power of the keys" such as is claimed by the Pontiffs of Rome; or the Protestant hierarchy along the line of "Apostolic Succession", or even the Independent churches in the matter of ecclesiastical authority and discipline. No, Peter's keys are not keys of the

human ecclesia or organized church: Peter's keys are keys of the divine ecclesia of God's spiritual Kingdom.[3]

Two years later he wrote a sequel to *The Kingdom* simply titled *The Church*. It was published January 1, 1901. In it he affirms the essential role of Kingdom life creating Church life. He realizes an interlocking role of the Kingdom and the Church. One of his comprehensive statements offers a summary of our mission:

> We must, for example, substitute today for yesterday; adjustment for tradition; witnessing for speculating; rallying for scattering; ministering for officering; enthusiasm for exactitude; hospitality for prejudgment; forestalling for improvising; good news for dogma; common sense for castle building; buttressing for criticising; beneficence for benevolence; "Kingdom" for churchism; in short Christ for church....[4]

Knowing my eye sight was going to be limited for a time and possibly never fully restored, I "crammed" as much reading as possible into my wait for the surgery described in the first chapter. These two Boardman books were among those I absorbed, along with three books by Bob Roberts and a few others I had been waiting to read. So in that facedown position my mind had plenty to process and my heart was full of Christ's promised presence.

THE BLUEPRINTS FOR KINGDOM OPERATIVES

The invisible is more real than the visible. God's Kingdom is invisible. Out of the invisible the visible has come, but the invisible is more real.

> *He is the image of the invisible God, the firstborn over all creation. For by Him all things were created: things in heaven and on earth, visible and invisible, whether thrones or powers or rulers or authorities; all things were created by Him and for Him. He is before all things, and in Him all things hold together. And He is the head of the body, the church; He is the beginning and the firstborn from among the dead, so that in everything He might have the supremacy. For God was pleased to have all His fullness dwell in Him, and through Him to recon-cile to Himself all things, whether things on earth or things in heaven, by making peace through His blood, shed on the cross* (Colossians 1:15-20 NIV).

The image of the invisible God has become visible in Christ. All God's fullness dwells in Him, and He makes Heaven and earth interactive through His shed blood and His life given on the cross.

I will declare it again: His Kingdom becomes visible with Him. The clearer we see Him, the clearer we see the Kingdom.

I am deliberately not trying to define all of the aspects of Kingdom expressions. Large numbers of model churches do not exist who have a Kingdom perspective and understanding across America, but more churches are beginning to explore Kingdom directives. I am going to suggest five basic realms of Kingdom experience:

1. The Individual—The Kingdom is within us. As body, soul, and spirit, we are to be Spirit-filled and Spirit-led. We are spirit beings with souls and bodies. Spirit-led people realize that the Kingdom starts within us, but does not stop there.

2. The Family—Family life is the first corporate expression of Kingdom life. Every house becomes an embassy for ambassadors who represent another Kingdom. Years ago, I was invited to the U.S. Embassy in Delhi, India. We drove through the impoverished conditions of that city, where people even lived in the large concrete sewer pipes that had yet to be buried. The smelly stench of open sewage and the unkempt conditions of their capital city ended when we entered the U.S. Embassy. Air-conditioned comfort greeted us, along with the smell of cleanliness. U.S. Marines stood guard, and specially trained hosts greeted us with drinks and

snacks. The wealth of another kingdom was evidenced from the street entrance throughout the entire complex. Such an expression of life ordered and provided for by another Kingdom is the right we have as Kingdom families.

3. The Church—Going to church was once called going to the house of God. God does have a house, but it is not a building. He once had a tent and then a temple where His glory dwelt for a time. But as Christ He moved into a body and walked in it for 33 years. Following the ascension of Christ, He moved into 120 people, making them Christ's Body. Soon the number increased to 3,000 and then 5,000 more. The Church, defined as His Body, is a Kingdom location.

4. The City Church—No one church can meet the needs of an area. All of the Body of Christ of that area makes up a Kingdom overlay for city strategy. Churches are not competitors, but partners doing Kingdom business. Walls of church separation fall in the light of Kingdom unity in the midst of diversity. Kingdom life is creative. Many flavors of church life grow out of the city church,

and God likes all of the flavors of Kingdom blends.

5. The Neighborhood—Neighborhoods make up our nation. Each neighborhood has a personality unique to that particular location. Many factors combine to create the community personality, such as ethnicity, income, median age, religious beliefs, and education. Most of the neighborhoods across America are so nondescript they have no names, though some communities have been named and become well-known, such as Queens or Watts. For most, their identity is a zip code. They are made up of people wanting to enjoy life, provide for their families, and pursue their dreams.

Every person in every neighborhood is important to the Lord. They all also have the same God-shaped space in their lives waiting to be filled with the presence of Christ. God may show up disguised as our neighbor, waiting to see if we'll care about Him. Jesus found material needs and spiritual needs inseparable. He said that when people give water to the thirsty, they are giving it to Him (see Matt. 10:42). Mother Teresa said, "When once more Christ came in distressing disguise, in the hungry man, the lonely man, in the homeless child and those seeking shelter."[5] When Amy Carmichael was criticized for her humanitarian work in India, she said, "One cannot save and then pitchfork souls into heaven. Souls are more or less fastened to bodies and you cannot get the souls out and deal with them separately. You have to take them both together."[6]

When we discover God's heart for all people, our own hearts begin to embrace His ways of being engaged in their lives. It is likely that God disguises Himself as a neighbor and actually lives in our neighborhood, hoping we will visit Him.

Helping a neighbor is difficult until we can find the neighbor. The question, "Who is my neighbor?" has long been an issue. Jesus was asked that same question 1,900 years ago. When the issue of how we obtain eternal life arose, Jesus gave a provocative answer. Here is the account framed in modern language by Eugene Peterson in The Message:

Just then a religion scholar stood up with a question to test Jesus. "Teacher, what do I need to do to get eternal life?" He answered, "What's written in God's Law? How do you interpret it?" He said, "That you love the Lord your God with all your passion and prayer and muscle and intelligence—and that you love your neighbor as well as you do yourself."

*"Good answer!" said Jesus. "Do it and you'll
live." Looking for a loophole, he asked, "And
just how would you define 'neighbor'?" Jesus
answered by telling a story. "There was once
a man traveling from Jerusalem to Jericho.
On the way he was attacked by robbers. They
took his clothes, beat him up, and went off
leaving him half-dead. Luckily, a priest was
on his way down the same road, but when he
saw him he angled across to the other side.
Then a Levite religious man showed up; he
also avoided the injured man. A Samaritan
traveling the road came on him. When he
saw the man's condition, his heart went out
to him. He gave him first aid, disinfecting
and bandaging his wounds. Then he lifted
him onto his donkey, led him to an inn,
and made him comfortable. In the morning
he took out two silver coins and gave them
to the innkeeper, saying, 'Take good care of
him. If it costs any more, put it on my bill—
I'll pay you on my way back.' What do you
think? Which of the three became a neighbor
to the man attacked by robbers?" "The one
who treated him kindly," the religion scholar
responded. Jesus said, "Go and do the same"*
(Luke 10:25-37 MSG).

A neighbor, according to Jesus Christ, is not just a person
next door or a person who lives nearby. He saw a neighbor

as a person with a need that He or others could meet. My neighbors are all the people I know of who can be assisted by my words, my deeds, or my actions on their behalf. When I become aware of their needs, they become my neighbors. When the person traveling a familiar road to Jericho from Jerusalem became aware of a man left by robbers in a ditch, he became his neighbor.

"Howdy, neighbor," may be a start toward assisting them. But our "Howdys" or "Hellos" are not enough to really change people or their circumstances. We may know these people, or we may be meeting them for the first time. My neighbors are those whom I am aware of that my knowledge and resources can assist. Peter and John could declare to a cripple, "We don't have gold or silver for your cup but what we have we will share with you. In the name of Jesus Christ of Nazareth stand up and walk" (see Acts 3:6). He did walk. Jesus gave him legs, and Peter took him by the hand and pulled him up. The supernatural and the practical combined.

One of the most respected men I have every known was Dr. Ernest Byers, medical doctor of Fort Worth, Texas. We were close friends and fellow elders in our church. I asked him one day what he would do if he was dressed formally to attend an important occasion and he drove up to the scene of a serious car wreck. Making the issue even more complex, I suggested that an injured person was still in the car needing immediate medical attention. How involved would he get? Would he get in the car to assist if it meant getting his clothes dirty or even tearing them in order to get to the person? What if he would have to spend so much time attending to the injured that he would miss the social function altogether?

He studied my face intently and weighed my words carefully. His eyes pierced my eyes as if he was reading a text on my soul. In his usual forthrightness and thoughtfulness, he answered without hesitation. He said, "Yes, I would stop at the wreck. I took the Hippocratic Oath to use my medical knowledge to save lives."

Knowing him, I was not surprised at his answer. The issue I was wrestling with then and still wrestle with several years later is, "Will I stop to help people whose lives are wrecked and need the nurturing I am capable of offering?"

It was during that same period of my life that my neighborhood increased in Fort Worth, Texas, to include all of the city. There were areas of the inner city that I had never considered my neighborhood. As I began visiting with people in those areas, I felt like I was stepping off a plane in another country. Stopping at wrecks changed my life.

Wrecks of many kinds await our attention. People are trapped in addictions and spiritual bondage. Many are wounded from wrecks in business, in church life, in family life, and in their own estrangement from God. We have the option of stopping at the wreck or waiting for the traffic to clear so we can drive away.

Jesus did more than identify our neighbors in academic terms. He certainly answered the question of a man who was testing Him. Our neighbors are the people in need whom we can help. But Jesus did more than give an answer. His very life was an illustration of the principle. The neighborhood where He had lived was a long way from the man He was answering.

He had entered a new time zone as He stepped out of eternity to dress up in the plain clothes of a man. Wearing plain clothes attire, He moved from place to place meeting needs. He went about doing good and healing the hurting.

> *And no doubt you know that God anointed Jesus of Nazareth with the Holy Spirit and with power. Then Jesus went around doing good and healing all who were oppressed by the Devil, for God was with Him* (Acts 10:38 NLT).

Wherever there was a need, Jesus saw that person as His neighbor. Even in His greatest anguish, He identified a thief dying next to Him on the cross as His neighbor. His neighborhood was the place where people in need were found. Finding them is one step. Sharing with them is the next step.

SUPPLIES FROM HEAVEN IN THE GENERAL STORE

Our neighbors have needs. We have supplies. We have supplies because Jesus made us joint heirs in this family business of Kingdom life. When Jesus described the remarkable operation called the Kingdom of God, He said,

> *Then you see how every student well-trained in God's kingdom is like the owner of a general store who can put his hands on anything you need, old or new, exactly when you need it* (Matthew 13:52 MSG).

As managers of the Kingdom business on this earth, we operate out of the "General Store." Some of our shelves may not carry the inventory we have access to in the warehouse of Heaven. That is why it is necessary to keep Heaven and earth interactive.

The General Store was part of my experience growing up in southern Missouri. Everything from soup to nails could be found there. Food for farm animals was paid for across the same counter where we purchased our food for the family. In the winter, the store's pot-bellied stove was a place to visit, to have fellowship, and to catch up on all the news of the neighborhood.

From our General Store we may offer love, friendship, advice, and encouragement. A formidable talent pool assembles in this store every day. From the shelves we may be placing goods in people's hands to assist with items for their home, for their food, or for their clothing. Or we may get on the phone to Heaven's warehouse calling for physical healing, mental healing, or spiritual healing. This general store is the biggest store on this earth. It far exceeds Wal-Mart in its size and number of locations. It is the General Store of Kingdom enterprises.

THE KINGDOM IS COMING

When our eyes see Jesus and His Kingdom, we have found the pearl of great price (see Matt. 13:46). It is time to sell everything and seek first this Kingdom. Selling all to seek the Kingdom doesn't leave us empty-handed or empty-hearted. All the other things will be added to us, including a heart full of vision and anticipation.

We are poised near unprecedented visitations of God. A stirring in people's hearts is occurring everywhere. People are lifting their heads and asking, "What is that sound I am hearing?" It is the sound of His Kingdom coming. All that is waiting is for our lives to be filled again with faith.

In the book *A Savior for all Seasons,* there is an account of a college president who was a true visionary. He had stayed in the home of a church Bishop who thought he was an expert on far more than church government. He expounded on one of his theories, that they were near the end of the century and everything of significance had been discovered that would ever be discovered.

The college president disagreed and said he believed that one day men would fly. The Bishop, whose last name was Wright, said "If God wanted us to fly He would have given us wings." Though Bishop Wright had little faith for flying, He had two sons named Orville and Wilbur. They had a greater vision than their father. Their craft was pretty crude and their flight was pretty short, but they flew.[7]

Florence Chadwick tried to swim from Catalina Island to the shore of California. After 15 hours, she asked to be taken from the water. She had swum the English Channel both ways and was within a half mile of reaching the California coast. It was a foggy day, and she could not see the shore. Later she said, "I'm not excusing myself, but if I could have seen the land I might have made it."[8] It wasn't the cold or fear or exhaustion that caused Florence Chadwick to fail, it was limited vision.

Our limited vision can be corrected quickly if we turn again to Jesus and allow Him to touch us. John's Gospel gives a detailed account of a man receiving sight who had been born blind. Creativity is never lacking with Jesus. He rubbed mud in the man's eye sockets and told him to go wash in a nearby pool. When the mud was washed out, the blindness was washed away as well (see Luke 9:6-7). Jesus did not rub the blindness in the man's eyes, but He did rub the mud in to cause him to act in faith. He did not give us our blindness, either. Whatever He may rub into our lack of sight will be an exercise to assist us to act in faith. There is much in our eyes that needs to be washed out.

When H.G. Wells, the famous historian, encountered the truth about the Kingdom of God, he wrote:

> Why here is the most radical proposal ever presented to the mind of man, the proposal to replace the present world order with God's order, the Kingdom of God.[9]

Wells is right about "the most radical proposal ever presented to the mind of man." Such a transformational truth requires that the mind must either welcome the proposal or refuse it. A radical proposal requires a radical response. There is no room for a casual consideration of Kingdom implications.

When God's 400 years of silence was broken, He called for a radical response. Just as a pause in music is part of the musical score, God's pause before speaking again was part of His plan to punctuate a statement. God's pause, the absence of a prophetic voice for 400 years, was intended to signal the significance of the next word He gave. That first word spoken after 400 years was "repent" (see Matt. 3:2).

When He spoke again, He chose a unique vessel named John the Baptist. Jesus declared he was the greatest person born of natural birth. Yet Jesus also said the least in the Kingdom of God is greater than he (see Matt. 11:11). John the Baptist was the instrument to end the silence of God.

The message was clear and concise, *"Repent, for the kingdom of God is at hand"* (see Matt. 4:17). A worthy response was required. Repentance was the only proper response to someone coming to lead a revolutionary way of life. Repentance is the only appropriate response to something so monumental as the Kingdom coming to us. We cannot accommodate the Kingdom as being equal to our other values and commitments. Seeking *first* the Kingdom is an essential element of repentance. Whatever else we have looked to and embraced, we must turn away from it in order to embrace the rule of Christ in His Kingdom.

Repentance is the essential response that allows Christ's rule within us. For too long, repentance has been seen as a negative reaction to get rid of something bad. It is, in fact, a gift God grants to us so we can turn to the greatest experience He offers us.

Our minds and wills become the hinges that open to receive the King and His Kingdom. This greatest proposal ever presented to the mind of man means we are His gates and doors of entry. He will come to us, and if welcomed, He will come through us to establish His rule on this earth. David understood the role of gates and doors allowing the King of glory to come.

Lift up your heads, O you gates; be lifted up,
you ancient doors, that the King of glory may

come in. Who is this King of glory? The Lord
strong and mighty, the Lord mighty in battle.
Lift up your heads, O you gates; lift them
up, you ancient doors, that the King of glory
may come in. Who is He, this King of glory?
The Lord Almighty—He is the King of glory
(Psalm 24:7-10 NIV).

Our lives are the doors through which He comes as the King of glory. We also become gates for His entrance into cities and regions to create an order of life which expresses His rule.

Of those who have thrown wide the gates of their lives to receive the King of glory and His attending Kingdom, none that I know have welcomed Him more than Jack Taylor. For at least a decade, he has declared the Kingdom, demonstrated the Kingdom, and deposited seed thoughts in others for Kingdom enlargement. Without his faithful friendship and encouragement, this book would not exist. I have received his permission to share from his pen as succinct a statement as I have ever read on the magnitude of the Kingdom. Watch out and make room because it is like the tiny mustard seed that becomes a giant tree from which will grow a forest of reality. It is a fitting ending to this book.

THE KINGDOM

It's bigger than we thought.

It's bigger than we can think.

It's bigger than we can imagine.

Too big to fit into anything because it is everything.

Anything that is a valid part of the whole fits into everything.

You can have everything outside the Kingdom and have nothing!

You can have the Kingdom and nothing else and have everything.

Time, life, light, space, eternity, the cosmos and all else are parts

Of the whole.

The whole is greater than the sum of its individual parts.

Only when we assess the individual parts within and in relationship with the whole do we see their deepest meaning, assess their highest value, and discover how and where they fit in the whole Kingdom scheme.

Each part is corrected, crowned, and correlated according to the template of all Kingdom truth.

Only in the Kingdom do we discover the key to the balance of

Knowing and being,

Declaring and demonstrating,

Thinking and acting,

Dying and living,

The divine event and the divine process,

All of this within the eternal government of love.

The end.[10]

Endnotes

INTRODUCTION

1. "God Is Alive," *West Plains Daily Quill* (Friday, Nov 11, 1966), front page.

CHAPTER 1

1. Helen Keller, www.brainyquote.com.

2. I heard Dr. Bill Hogue, Secretary of Evangelism for the Southern Baptist Convention, make these comments in various settings.

CHAPTER 3

1. Bob Roberts, *Glocalization* (Grand Rapids, MI: Zondervan, 2007), 34.

2. *Ibid.,* 42.

CHAPTER 4

1. Richard F. Lovelace, *Dynamics of Spiritual Life* (Downers Grove, IL: InterVarsity Press, 1979), 19.

2. Billy Graham, 1979. Although I was not present at this meeting, one of the men who attended it shared with me the events that he witnessed at this event.

3. I was in meetings with Bill Bright and other leaders at San Bernardino, California, in such discussions.

CHAPTER 5

1. J. Sidlow Baxter, *Divine Healing* (Grand Rapids, MI: Zondervan, 1979), 180.

2. Taken from transcriptions of a lecture given by Dr. Donald A. McGavran.

3. Darren Wilson, producer and director, *The Finger of God*, DVD (Chicago: Wanderlust Productions, 2007), segment on Heidi Baker.

4   Dr. Fred Hubbs, "Healed of Intense Pain," *Fulness* magazine (November/December 1983), 21-22.

5. A.W. Tozer, *Wingspread: A.B. Simpson: A Study in Spiritual Altitude* (Camp Hill, PA: Wingspread Publishers, 1988).

6. Win Arn, *The Pastor's Manual for Effective Ministry*, Monrovia, CA. Church Growth, 1988), 26

7. Kaiser EDU.Org. estimates that 45 million are uninsured.

CHAPTER 6

1. Charles G. Finney, www.historymatters.gmu.edu /d/6374/.

2. Peter Marshall and David Manuel, *The Light and the Glory* (Old Tappan, NJ: Fleming H. Revell, 2007), 235-236.

3. See, for example, Dr. Neil Anderson, *Victory Over Darkness: Realizing the Power of Your Identity in Christ* (Ventura, CA: Regal Books/Gospel Light Press, 2000), *The Bondage Breaker* (Eugene, OR: Harvest Home Publishers, 2000), and *Winning Spiritual Warfare* (Eugene, OR: Harvest Home Publishers, 1991), all of which can be found on Amazon.com.

4. Marshal and Manuel, 235.

5. Mark I. Bubeck, *The Adversary* (Chicago, IL: Moody Press, 1975), 9-10.

CHAPTER 7

1. Gene Edwards, *A Tale of Three Kings* (Goleta, CA: Christian Books, 1980).

2. Gene Edwards, *Our Mission* (Augusta, ME: Christian Books, 1980), 17.

3. Gene Edwards, *A Tale of Three Kings* (Goleta, CA: Christian Books, 1980), 22, 27-28.

CHAPTER 8

1. E. Stanley Jones, *The Unshakable Kingdom and the Unchanging Person* (Nashville, TN: Abingdon Press, 1972), 34.

2. *Ibid.*, 15.

3. Robert Lewis, *The Church of Irresistible Influence* (Grand Rapids, MI: Zondervan, 2001).

4. Bob Buford, *Half Time* (Grand Rapids, MI: Zondervan, 1997).

5. Hannah Whitall Smith, *The Christian's Secret of a Happy Life* (Chicago: Moody Publishers, 2009).

CHAPTER 9

1. Taken from "Dreams and Visions Move Muslims to Christ," Posted in True Stories by National and International Religion Report, http://www.epm.org/artman2/publish/missions_true_stories/Dreams_Visions_Move_Muslims_to_Christ.shtml.

2. Dallas Willard, *The Divine Conspiracy* (San Francisco: Harper One, 1998).

3. *Ibid.*,80.

CHAPTER 10

1.　Mother Theresa, see www.memorablequotations.com /mother.htm.

2.　Darren Wilson, producer and director, *Finger of God,* DVD (Chicago: Wanderlust Productions, 2007).

3.　Heidi Baker, *Always Enough* (Grand Rapids, MI: Chosen Books, 2003), 19.

4.　See C.S. Lewis, Miracles (New York: HarperCollins Publishers, 2000; first published 1947), 1-4.

CHAPTER 11

1.　Henry Blackaby, *Experiencing God* (Nashville: Life Way Press, 2007), 16.

2.　Craig Goreschel at The Catalyst Conference 2007, given in a series of sermons titled "The Practical Atheist." See Craig Goreschel, *The Christian Atheist* (Grand Rapids, MI: Zondervan, 2010).

3.　Robert Frost, "The Road Not Taken," *Mountain Interval* (New York: Henry Holt and Company, 1920), ll. 18-20.

4.　International Standard Bible Encyclopedia, "tribulation," http://www.internationalstandardbible.com/T/tribulation .html.

5.　Charles G. Finney, See www. historymatters.gmu.edu /d/6374/.

6.　Karl Barth, quoted in Romano Penna, *Paul the Epostle: Wisdom and Folly of the Cross* (Collegeville, MN: Liturgical Press, 1996), 200.

7.　Bob Roberts, *Real Time Connections* (Grand Rapids, MI: Zondervan, 2010,), 208, 209.

Chapter 12

1.   Richard G. Kyle, *The Last Days Are Here Again: A History of the End Times* (Ada, MI: Baker Publishing Group, 1998).

Chapter 13

1.   R.T. Kendall, *In Pursuit of His Glory* (Lake Mary, FL: Charisma House, 2004), 264.

2.   *Ibid.,* 2-3.

3.   *Ibid.,* 71.

4.   *Ibid.,* 81.

5.   *Ibid.,* 93.

6.   *Ibid.,* 207.

7.   Bob Roberts, *Real Time Connections* (Grand Rapids, MI: Zondervan, 2010), 220.

8.   John Piper, *Let The Nations Be Glad* (Grand Rapids, MI: Baker Book House, 2003), 17.

Chapter 14

1.   Richard Stearns, *The Hole in Our Gospel* (Nashville, TN: Thomas Nelson, 2009).

2.   *Ibid.,* 18.

3.   *Ibid.,* 16.

4.   Ed Stetzer, shared in a message given at Northwood Church, Keller, Texas, November 1, 2009.

5.   George Barna, *Revolution* (Wheaton, IL: Tyndale House, 2005), 2, 3.

6.   Neil Cole, *Organic Leadership* (Grand Rapids, MI: Baker Book House, 2009), 41.

7.   *Ibid.,* 40.

8.   Stearns, 26.

9. Ron Hall and Denver Moore with Lynn Vincent, *Same Kind of Different as Me* (Nashville, TN: Thomas Nelson, 2006).

10. Biblesoft Hymnal, PC Study Bible electronic database Copyright © 2003 by Biblesoft, Inc. All rights reserved.

CHAPTER 15

1. Gene Mims, *Thine Is The Kingdom* (Nashville, TN: LifeWay Press,1997), 18.

2. George Dana Boardman, *The Kingdom: The Emerging Rule of Christ Among Men,* Bob Mumford and Jack Taylor, compilers (Shippensburg, PA: Destiny Image Publishers, 2008), 311.

3. *Ibid.,* [[**ED: These endnotes appeared to be misnumbered. I believe this should be Ibid but don't know page number. Paginator]]**

4. George Dana Boardman, *The Church: The Divine Ideal,* Bob Mumford and Jack Taylor, compilers (Shippensburg, PA: Destiny Image Publishers, 2008), 64.

5. Mother Theresa, www.memorablequotations.com/mother .htm.

6. Frank Houghton, *Amy Carmichael of Dohnavur* (London: Society for the Propagation of Christian Knowledge, 1954), 213.

7. William Pierson Barker, *A Savior for all Seasons* (Grand Rapids, MI: Fleming H. Revell, 1986); see "For the Love of Flying," http://blog.sportflyingfriends.

8. Brian Cavanaugh, *Fresh Packet of Sowing Seeds* (Third Planting), (Mahwah, NJ: Paulist Press, 1994).

9. H.G. Wells, quoted in E. Stanley Jones, *The Unshakeable Kingdom and the Unchanging Person* (Nashville, TN: Abingdon Press, 1972), 11.

10. Jack Taylor, personal-mail attachment, March 29, 2009.

MINISTRY PAGE

To contact Jim Hylton you can email him at:

www.supernaturalskyline.com

or

jim@supernaturalskyline.com